BOOKS BY CALVIN RUTSTRUM

Way of the Wilderness
The New Way of the Wilderness
The Wilderness Cabin
North American Canoe Country
The Wilderness Route Finder
Paradise Below Zero
Greenhorns in the Southwest
Challenge of the Wilderness
Once Upon a Wilderness

ONCE UPON A WILDERNESS

CALVIN RUTSTRUM

Once Upon a Wilderness

ILLUSTRATIONS BY THE AUTHOR

The Macmillan Company, New York, New York
Collier-Macmillan Publishers, London

ACKNOWLEDGMENTS

THE AUTHOR wishes to thank:

The U.S. Fish and Wildlife Service of Anchorage, Alaska, for use of the red fox, Barren Ground caribou, Arctic tern, rock ptarmigan, and bald eagle photos; and Mrs. Carl Frank of Rochester, Minnesota, for the photo of the geese—all in Chapter 17.

The Macmillan Company
866 Third Avenue, New York, N.Y. 10022
Collier-Macmillan Canada Ltd., Toronto, Ontario

Library of Congress Catalog Card Number: 72-91260
First Printing

Printed in the United States of America

Contents

1   The Wilderness Today   *1*

2   The Earlier Approach   *11*

3   Then and Now by
    Comparison   *23*

4   Wilderness Happy   *37*

5   The Inner Man Yesterday
    and Today   *58*

6   Thoreau—An Afflatus   *68*

7   Hands and Feet Upon the
    Wilderness   *78*

8   Women in the Wilderness   *91*

9   The Alien Wilderness   *100*

10 The Micro-Wilderness   *106*

11 Legend of a Woodsman   *112*

12 Wilderness Sanctuary   *121*

13 No Tale Will Tell   *133*

14 Solitude   *141*

15 Burning Bridges Behind   *149*

16 Nostalgia   *158*

17 The Wilderness
    Tomorrow   *168*

ONCE UPON A WILDERNESS

"... *the clearing process following a three-day rain* ..."

1. The Wilderness Today

P L A C E: Marchington Lake, Northern Ontario, Canada; West
Longitude 91° 28′ 10″—North Latitude 50° 10′ 30″.
T I M E: Autumn.
H A B I T A T: A tiny studio cabin set prominently out on the
Precambrian, rockbound, peninsular shore some fifty feet
from the main living cabin.

AS I TYPE these pages, a Franklin fireplace stove, burning jackpine and birch, warms my back enough to allow a
wide-open door at a temperature well under sixty degrees. A
moderately heavy sea pounds the shore—the clearing process
following a three-day rain, though billowing rain-cloud masses
still continue to roll up from the northwest that seem to
threaten a shower. They are, I find, merely the tailings of
yesterday's downpour and speedily disappear on a scudding,

dry run over the southeast forest. Through window and door I see island beyond island, mile upon mile of unpeopled, coniferous-timbered shore.

The general tenor of the foregoing may suggest isolation—even remoteness—but a few revealing facts should prove this to be more apparent than real. At the near shore rests a Prospector model aluminum canoe, which can readily take my wife and me two miles to a mere wilderness railroad siding on the Canadian National Railroad where a local train could by signal be induced to stop—if one were sufficiently patient in putting up with currently bad train schedules. Though mail and provisions come to us by rail only once a week, the railroad is, nevertheless, the umbilical cord that ties us to a material-conscious, overpopulated, outside world. Further to prove that my wife and I live in apparent but not real isolation, a chartered pontoon-equipped plane in summer or ski-equipped plane in winter can by radio telephone be procured that in the span of half an hour, cruising at 120 miles per hour, carries us to the much-vaunted outside world. Of course, when we choose, and on occasion we choose, it can alternately take us deeper into Canada's wilderness.

A Chicago sports fisherman who visited this area and had a sudden attack of appendicitis pointed out that he reached a hospital by pontoon-equipped plane from this wilderness area quicker than he could have reached a hospital by car or ambulance from his residence in his own home city of Chicago.

One might presume from this ample means of access that the approximately three hundred million people on the North American continent would find no obstacles to their encroachment upon the vast remaining wilderness areas. Obviously and fortunately they do find obstacles. In this fact the wilderness devotees can probably take some solace. With the existing, described, available transportation to our cabin area, it will be of interest to note that the total obtrusion in the last few days by America's millions of people has amounted to a small fishing party departing from the camp at the west end of

"At the near shore rests a Prospector model aluminum canoe . . ."

the lake, and a father and son combination passing by on a canoe voyage.

What essentially, we might ask, is the inhibiting factor behind this seeming "wall of inaccessibility" that manages to close out the continent's vast population from the wilderness? The primary factor here, of course, is that as metal filings rush to the magnet, so, fortunately, does the lure of cities attract most of the population, a social circumstance that must rank first in delaying inroads upon the wilderness.

The canoe route to our cabin, twenty-five miles from the nearest wilderness settlement, calls for one long portage or two shorter ones around rapids and falls. These few portages also have proved to be obstacles enough to screen out all but the occasional wilderness canoe tripper. Fishermen and hunters in small numbers do, of course, find their way here by chartered plane or poor rail service, but they remain only for a short time. Long intervals occur when no one comes at all, and solitude reigns again.

The pontoon plane in open water and the ski plane in win-

ter, along with the snowmobile, naturally seem discouragingly
incursive to many who seek to keep the wilderness inviolate;
but these inroads are of short duration. Snowmobiles, though
numerous, are largely confined to towns and the immediate
outlying areas. It is true, of course, that you could, if necessary, set down a wheelchair-confined invalid on most any
wilderness spot in the world by plane or helicopter. That is,
you might presume to do so as a transport possibility—or, at
least, seem to accomplish it in tenable transportation theory.
Bear in mind, however, that it costs between one and two
dollars per mile to charter a plane to any significantly remote
wilderness area.

For the average budget this cost repeated as a recreational
pattern would be quite an economic hurdle. If expense proves
no object, then consider the typical nature of the affluent few
who can afford to undertake such ventures. Most often they
are the product of business or industrial fretfulness, generally
a restless lot who remain briefly in an area and "fish their fool
heads off." Morning to night fishing is primarily what they
must have to satisfy their industrially addicted reflexes. Soon
—fish-satiated and fish-pound glutted—they depart, having in-
flicted by their short stay some—but not serious—harm on the
wilderness. Encroachment by plane upon the wilderness is
sporadic and short-lived, and, thus, should not trouble those
with sensitive wilderness sentiment.

To highly wilderness-conscious people, of course, the mere
appearance of a plane a few thousand feet above a remote
wilderness area is painfully disturbing.

In the early literary archives I recall in point an account of
two pioneers in soiled, well-worn buckskin shirts, sitting on
the bank of the Missouri River, seeing the first steamboat in
the river's history plying its upstream course. The two men
cursed its appearance and proclaimed that the wilderness was
"shot to hell." On a particular seven weeks' canoe journey in
Canada's wilds, I tended to agree with a trail-worn prospector
whom I met in the interior, when in our conversation I asked

"*. . . prolonged cold rain, turning to snow . . .*"

him about the incursion upon the wilds. "My God, man," he said, "there's plenty of bush."

There are, we can be sure, more inhibiting circumstances to excessive inroads upon the wilderness areas than common speculation reveals. At this juncture, I have observed through the open door of my studio cabin a sudden changed direction and increase in the wind velocity that is kicking up a heavy sea. White thrashing breakers send spray ten feet or more up on the shore—a condition that usually keeps the arriving canoe tripper unembarked, or, if he is under way, keeps him windbound and concerned over trip-time loss. Scarcely ever does the in-town anticipation or planning of a wilderness canoe journey include the usual crop of adversity that is actually harvested: prolonged cold rain, turning to snow; overgrown, obscure portage trails; inordinately rough and devious terrain; swarms of "man-eating" insects in the fly season; water levels that sometimes impede or even terminate travel during drought periods, while at other times creating complex flood conditions.

There are, of course, the serene days when camp is pitched on just the ideal shore, the sun casting oblique lightings that make photography and aesthetic gratification on reaching a campsite seem more important than the preparation of a past-due camp supper. Mornings can break so clear, calm and insect-free that the first awakening call of a loon over placid water starts a day of serenity, a measure of comfort and pleasure that the most idealistically preconceived canoe journey could scarcely visualize. The leisurely paddle along a rockbound, forested shore can, under these conditions, bring such inspiring surprises and memorable experiences as to leave them etched upon one's memory for life.

But such days are not the perpetual routine of the usual canoe voyage. Dawn may come too often in a saturated fog-gloom of "hung-dog" weather with leaden skies and dripping, soggy forests—a condition that can drag on with the possible end hopelessly projected day after day into unforeseeable future change. A prevailing wind from Hudson Bay can at such times usher in a temperature of thirty-eight degrees with rain, carrying with it a chill factor incomparable in discomfort to any other weather. Even breaking trail through deep snow with a dog team at thirty below has more to offer comfortwise.

In over a half century of wilderness travel, I have seen rough weather take its toll. Not in life and limb in most instances, though even this was a part of it, but the weather-beating of initial wilderness travelers which left only the hardy few among them returning for a repeat trip—those who learned to meet the elements with carefully calculated pre-trip planning, and on the trail, methodically sound daily routine derived from a lifetime habit of meeting and cheerfully resolving unusually difficult problems as integral parts of a life pattern.

We scarcely ever hear from those who in "quiet desperation" fear going into the wilderness at all for various reasons—some valid, some false. A common one of these for some is the legitimate fear of getting lost; the other a fallacious fear of being attacked by wild animals. Both of these deterrents to wilderness travel have, no doubt, played their own moderate part in preserving the wilderness.

But I am inclined to believe that the greatest inhibitor of rugged wilderness travel today is the growing enervation of body vigor, the condition of urbanized, modern, easy living. We have become in varying degrees what I might term too "comfortized." Few who manage a weekend or a two-week vacation-exposure to the outdoors ever stray very far from their cars. Hiking largely went out with the development of

"*. . . when camp is pitched on just the ideal shore . . .*"

the internal combustion engine. The complementary enervator, no doubt, is rich food in endless variety. Without ample exercise, excessive eating and drinking have brought on the early paunch and unmuscled legs. Habituate this debilitating physical process—the overeating and drinking—and you need have little to fear from populations invading the deeper, inner sanctum of the wilderness, at least by physically energetic means. And I repeat, the mechanized invaders soon depart.

Thus, a great wilderness remains. We haven't, of course, learned how to manage it intelligently, but if we can develop an industrial, social, and ecological sanity soon enough, perhaps the great areas of inviolate wilderness will remain a real-

ity. The most scientifically sound wilderness plan is to leave it undisturbed to perpetuate itself. The least sound in principle is the pseudoscience of "multiple use." If we carry on the fatuous premise that all wilderness areas must be "developed" —which, defined, has in the past invariably resulted in industrial ravage—the chances are imminently great that the forces of nature will destroy mankind before mankind wholly destroys the wilderness.

"Thus, a great wilderness remains."

"*A vast forested wilderness of lakes and rivers . . .*"

2. The Earlier Approach

IN RETROSPECT consider the approach to wilderness activity early in the century and before. A vast forested wilderness of lakes and rivers, of prairie and mountain, stretched across the northern and western United States, joined to the north by an adjacent, even greater, wilderness expanse in Canada. Here in these wilderness areas the strong, calloused, primeval hand of welcome was extended by nature to the adventurous spirit. But the invitation applied primarily to the qualified, the properly equipped, wherever they ventured deep into the wilds. To those so equipped and with a faculty for applying their knowledge and skill, the wilderness became generous and kindly. If they failed to meet these challenges, the wilderness took its toll.

Proper application of method and equipment did not rest on caprice, but on a kind of wilderness propriety, if not tradition. If wrong in choice or improper in application, the wilderness body rejected it, and as impersonally rejected the user.

We might have hoped in that era that selection of wilderness equipment and method had been worked out by such industries as were engaged in the business of practical supply, and that one needed only to make one's needs for wilderness travel known and these desires would be fulfilled. But this was not true near the beginning of the century, and in many respects it has become less true now.

Entering a sporting goods store, one would think that it would be possible to glean a knowledge of wilderness equipment and its suggested use. Today, a sporting goods store is more likely to feature floppy tourist hats, tobacco humidors, charcoal broilers, gold-studded collars, and super-duper-pooper-scoopers for pets, though a plethora of guns and fishing tackle is stocked. Early in the century there was, of course, a supply of golf clubs, tennis racquets, baseball and football gear. But these items did not predominate. Athletic shops garnered most of this business. Largely in sporting goods stores there were packsacks; tumplines; snowshoes; round-bottomed sailcloth food bags for carrying dry wilderness foods; rainshirts and sou'wester hats; larrigans; canoes and paddles; toboggans; stag shirts and mackinaw pants; sheath knives; nesting cook pails; wool underwear and socks—along, of course, with guns, fishing tackle, and the incidentals.

Yet, even in that earlier time, all of the proper items needed to get one off on an extensive canoe or dogsled journey were not in ready commercial supply. And to this day, it is almost impossible to organize and supply a properly equipped wilderness voyage without worldwide catalog-rummaging and the inescapable need for custom-making certain items. I have covered these points quite thoroughly in my currently published books, *The New Way of the Wilderness*, *North American Canoe Country*, and *Paradise Below Zero*, so I will use only a few suggestive references here to contrast the *then* and *now* approach.

The tumpline, for example, disappeared from the sporting goods store quite early. It was still available at Hudson's Bay

Company outpost supply depots up to a short time ago, but may largely have been discontinued. It consisted of a leather head strap to which two eight-foot by one-inch leather straps were sewed. To use it, several packs of camp equipment were bundled together with the straps, the whole load carried with the head strap resting on the fore part of the head, not on the forehead. The head position is important. It is in the right place when it feels right—a line of balanced support from head to foot.

Long use of the tumpline developed strong neck muscles. This was the portage trail packing method used by the Hudson's Bay Company through the early fur trade. Short, rather stocky men were hired for this job, and their carrying abilities have become traditional. Taller men were more susceptible to back trouble. At the Trappers' Festival at The Pas, Manitoba, Canada, I have seen contests where six hundred pounds and more of flour were carried with a tumpline. Winners were permitted to keep the flour as a prize. It was not unusual on Canadian portage trails in the early days to see tumpline loads

"The tumpline, for example . . ."

carried of about half this amount. Once the tumpline is used on portages for any considerable period, one is likely never to get away from its advantageous use. Even in the carrying of packsacks over portage trails, many find it more feasible to dispense with the shoulder straps and use only the head strap that is an integral part of the Poirer or Duluth packsack. (This head strap on packsacks is sometimes incorrectly called "the tumpline.")

Through the Canadian wilderness the method in earlier years for portaging a canoe was to use canoe paddles lashed across the thwarts of the canoe with a tumpline as a carrying yoke, the blades, sometimes padded, resting on one's shoulders, the head strap of the tumpline on one's head. Permanent spacing loops, properly positioned, were first lashed on the thwarts with a cord to receive the paddles, the paddles then securely lashed to the thwarts with the tumpline. This method is still used today by some canoe voyagers, especially by woods Indians and Eskimos.

Like many others, I suffer nostalgically by the discontinu-

Paddles used as a carrying yoke.

The graceful upsweep of the Peterborough toboggan.

ance of items that were once so much a part of early wilderness life. To recall the ruggedness of men carrying loads over portages with the tumpline, and to know that this mastery over the wilderness trails is vanishing, cannot help but leave a sense of voids. It was but a few years ago that the Peterborough toboggan, a beautiful item of equipment as the illustration will show, was also discontinued because of snowmobile competition. The upsweep of the forward part of this unit, so made to mount snowdrifts, gave the toboggan a graceful design that unfailingly caught the eye of the observer. There is a need for this unit today, but the individual woodsman will have to make his own, which could be a labor of love.

No personal material possessions have perhaps ever had greater romance and fascination than those associated with wilderness gear. Especially is this true if each item was bought with the qualifying, respectful knowledge of long-tradition practicability. For example, a packsack made in Duluth, Minnesota, could be bought which was rugged and practical, and to which sentiment could undoubtedly be attached. But if the budget allowed, the Abercrombie suppliers in New York could provide at a rather princely sum a deluxe type of packsack. The waterproofed canvas material used in the Abercrombie packsack was of high-grade sea-island cotton, dyed an attractive neutral color. The carrying straps were made of flexible, top-grain, latigo leather. The moment you saw and felt this pack you knew that here was prodigious design and quality; here could be the love of possession. If you cared to go a step further, Abercrombie stores had a packsack model with the edges of the canvas neatly trimmed in leather. Long use of these packs gave them an appearance of sophisticated mellowness which seemed to impart the maturity of the user. The owner came to enjoy their possession as a kind of wilderness status symbol.

The seasoned man of the wilderness got to know the route to travel when it came to buying equipment. He was not misguided by shoddy, gay commercialism. Leather boots did

not get into his camp outfit in any season unless they were strictly for an open-ground hiking trip. The seasoned woodsman, moreover, was never tripped up by such worthless items for the wilderness as air-impervious leather jackets that would soak him with perspiration condensation and chill him in a cold wind. He nevertheless knew the great value of a porous, Indian-tanned buckskin shirt, made from skins which had had the air-impervious grain removed. His shopping for wilderness equipment thus, inadvertently, had to snub many a clerk and bypass the cult of much currently consumed, ill-adapted, recreational merchandise. He slept in a rabbit-skin, fur, or down robe, and would have shunned the various synthetic-fiber robes imposed on the "modern" camper. There are many days in the northern wilderness in spring and autumn, even on occasion in summer, which demand a bed comparable to that for winter use—a fact many aspiring wilderness travelers fail to discover early enough.

Buying an outfit was thus no "shopping spree." Sources

Tracking lines were needed for "worrying" a canoe through a stretch of rapids. (Note man in rear carrying a sourdough pail.)

were widespread and diversified. There needed to be bought, for example, two braided-rope tracking lines several hundred feet long for "worrying" a canoe through a whitewater gorge, or up a stretch of rapids. These lines had to be treated with a mixture of melted beeswax and paraffin, dissolved in turpentine, with a little oil of tar for added strength, to prevent rot from frequent wetting, as well as to discourage gnawing by rodents. The blades of paddles had to be tapered to a narrower edge with a plane for increased efficiency of stroke, and then deep-soaked with a solution of tepid varnish, generously thinned with turpentine, to maintain the paddle shape against warping. There was the preseason order for a Prospector model canoe from Peterborough, Ontario, Canada, the canoe to be shipped months in advance to some point so that it would arrive in time for embarkation. It usually was found well cared for at the shipping destination in the warehouse of the Hudson's Bay Company, a point you reached by ship or rail. Some Scottish factor (manager) of the Hudson's Bay Company would likely meet you with a smile, and before you could ask about your canoe, he would call out:

"She's here, and a mighty fine craft she is."

A three-quarter-size cruiser ax was selected from the rack

"A three-quarter-size cruiser ax was selected . . ."

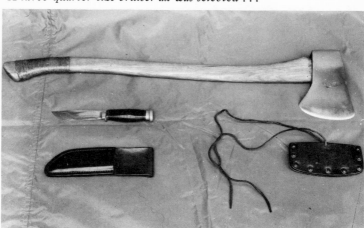

in a wilderness town hardware store, which was only a start, because you had to regrind the blade to thin it and then hone it to an edge sharper than Roquefort cheese; knock out the handle and reset it for perfect alignment, or replace it; make a leather sheath with a spring-brass lining; and tie it on the ax head with rawhide thongs. Short of this, it remained only a woodshed makeshift.

Thus, you ran the gamut of wide-range purchase and partial custom-remodeling of just about everything you carried with you into the wilds; and I repeat, this is, unfortunately, as true today as it was over fifty years ago. Redesigning and remodeling the wedge tent, as shown in the accompanying illustrations, provides an example. Running the tent flaps at both ends all the way to the ridge allowed raising either side of the tent to form a canopy to cook under in rain. Also, a mosquito netting the full size of the tent and suspended with loops inside the ridge gave protection from insects no matter what tent conversion was used. The mosquito netting quickly suspended away from the tent for a noonday stop avoided much insect trouble, or was needed for photographing wildlife from a blind. Before that revision, the wedge tent was much like all other nonconvertible tents—a fabric cell you crawled into to get out of the rain. The exception to this might be the commercially sold Baker type, designed for an open fire, and also the pyramid tent for the arctic winter.

When aluminum cooking kits followed the earlier copper-bottomed, heavily tinned, oval type, you had to discard (as you still do today) the aluminum cups and substitute a heavily tinned cup—now the stainless steel cup. Aluminum cups, because of their high heat conduction, were uncomfortably hot on your lips. You also discarded the aluminum frying pan because food stuck to it badly. The coating modern manufacturers put on pans to prevent sticking is short-lived on the wilderness camp-cook trail, though coatings more resistant to wear are being developed. Cooking kits still come with their share of useless items, and some of the cooking utensils now

"Running the tent flaps at both ends all the way to the ridge allowed raising either side of the tent to form a canopy . . ."

have no bails for hanging them over an open fire, being suitable only for the auto camp party with a stove.

Those not familiar with the true demands of the wilderness might believe that too much capriciousness is practiced in the choice of equipment. There was once less danger of pursuing that course than occurs in the case of modern equipment which by its purported sophistication can have a bad influence on practical selection. This became evident, for example, in the short, lever-action Winchester carbine, which in earlier times had become my choice in the need to live partly, and sometimes entirely, off the country. The carbine went with me on canoe voyage and dog sled trips, until the black finish was largely worn from it. The 44-40 shells of one model and the 30-30 shells of another could be bought at any store or Hudson's Bay Company Post on the continent. If desired, the 44-40 and 30-30 shells could as readily, in reverse, serve as

ABOVE: *Raising either tent-half provides a protective canopy.*

BELOW: *The mosquito netting can also be quickly suspended away from the tent.*

currency in these parts for buying provisions, or could be turned into cash.

One fall I guided a man who wanted to see and photograph moose. Though I had been well compensated for my services, I later found, in an express package he had sent to me, a fancy bolt-action rifle with telescope sight. On the next trip into the North I took it along instead of the carbine. It seemed at first an extraordinary and valuable acquisition. But because of its carrying clumsiness; its awkward additional length over the carbine; worst of all, the seeming fragility of the high-mounted scope, I found no place in the canoe or in camp where it could come to a safe, practical rest. I finally tired of babying it. A Hudson's Bay Post factor in the interior admired it. I sold it to him, receiving another 30-30 Winchester carbine and a substantial cash sum to boot. Now and then rain had to be poured out of the carbine barrel and drained from the action; at times the carbine got some unavoidable bumps; but a little drying and oiling in camp after adverse weather exposure, a resighting, and it was ready for the continuing journey, as integral with the canoe load and the portage pack as a canoe paddle.

In time one becomes knowledgeable about these things, and ample experience proves them over and over again. The element of uncertainty no longer dogs the wilderness traveler's tracks. A train sets one off at a railroad siding, or a ship anchors in the lee of a headland for one's shoreward canoe-embarkation point—or, as they say in the wilderness, the "jumping off place." At such eventful times, no troubled feelings, no apprehensions of not being able to cope with wilderness travel and living, prevail. The sharp corners of inexperience have long since worn off. Every piece of equipment falls into place. When the shore is reached and the captain gives a final, deep-throated, farewell blast from the ship's horn around the headland, a strange wilderness awaits, but strange only in geographical aspect, which delights and challenges.

3. Then and Now by Comparison

ॐ

PERHAPS the greatest urge to write these chapters was prompted by a young reader of my books who said, "I wish you would write a book on the wilderness as it was when you first knew it around the beginning of the century." He proceeded to explain that most people today do not know the wilderness at all, and those born within the last three or four decades who have had contact with the wilds in one degree or another cannot disassociate it from airplanes, outboard motors, snowmobiles, radios, and various other pseudo-pertinent gadgets, along with processed rather than staple foods, and no less the many inhibiting restrictions governing modern-day conduct in the wilderness.

If by magic a time-crank were handy to turn back the years, one wonders what of the modern world one would leave as it is, and what one would choose to crank out of existence.

For a single turn of the time-crank, I would like to have

back the profound mystery and enchantment that the earlier remoteness and seclusion of the wilderness offered. To this I might attach as a necessary component—adventure. Not misadventure in the sense that Vilhjalmur Stefansson defined it: "the result of incompetence," but, perhaps, as the encountering of unknown risks; bold exploratory ventures into strange regions; the meeting up with the rare and the primitive; heading up rivers, for example, which earlier were designated by mere conjectural dotted lines meandering into blank spaces on the map—whereas upon later, actual discovery, a magnificent unknown wilderness opened up to those who ventured into the "dotted line" region.

In all sincerity, I would crank out of existence the internal combustion engine, which tends to destroy profound wilderness values. Winston Churchill, as I have pointed out in a previous publication, suggested that the greatest misfortune to man, and he might have added *curse*, was the invention of the internal combustion engine.

What would happen if we actually did crank out of existence this both benevolent and infamous contraption? I can answer one phase of it by harking back to the earlier part of the century. In Minneapolis and St. Paul, where I spent much of my youth, a nickel took you by trolley line to the city limits, then not a very long ride, so generally you hiked to save the nickel. With a back pack you could set out from the end of the trolley line on a secluded and picturesque, motor-car-free, country road, which most often was but two meandering ruts through the forest. You could plan to be on the bank of some crystal-clear stream or on the shore of a clear-water lake before nightfall, to set up a small tent and cook your supper over a tiny wood fire. No outboard motor stirred up the water or broke the magic stillness; no plane roared overhead. A deep serenity came over the evening camp. An owl hooted, a whippoorwill called in his typical repetitive manner, and sleep was allowed to be couched in sweet repose.

Another kind of early-century trip I remember most distinctly. I had taken the train fifty miles to spend the summer with a cousin on my uncle's farm. It was a small farm on the shore of a lake where the pressures of agricultural economy seemed, as I recall them now, not very urgent. There was enough for a rainy day without obsessive hoarding. One lived along. My cousin's older brother had a reputation for making regular camping trips. I was invited to go along on the next one.

Into a wagon was loaded a heavy canvas wall tent with a complement fly (tarpaulin) as a second roof, along with a full-size wood-burning cook stove; a flat-bottom boat and oars; a two-man, eight-foot, crosscut saw; bedsprings; sawhorses and planks for a table; kerosene lanterns; boxes for seats in which the grub, cooking utensils, and water buckets were packed. Also taken were sacked oats and hay for the horses, and even an additional tarpaulin to be stretched between trees under which the horses could be stabled against rain and the direct sun—to some people, a seeming equine luxury. Every moment of it was exciting, from the loading of the ponderous gear to the harnessing of the horses. The three of us sat side by side on a wide, single-board, spring seat that rose rather dizzily, I thought, several feet higher than the horses' backs.

There was a majesty, nevertheless, about sitting up there. It was scenically strategic for view, and the whole, it seemed then, was frighteningly mobile. Boulders that had been too large for convenient removal from the road bed were bumped over noisily, and I thought precariously, by the heavy, steel-tired wheels. Now and then, a tree fallen across the road was by-passed or had to be cut out for further access with the two-man, eight-foot, crosscut saw. If the fallen tree was dead and of such sound wood that it would make good dry fuel, it was cut up and thrown on the wagon for later firewood.

I was intrigued by the various parts of the harness; the crupper that went under the horse's tail; the breeching straps that tightened up against the horse's buttocks as we went down the hills; the tightening of the traces and chains as we went up the hills, or were pulled out of some mudhole—a feat that called for a strenuous tug by the horses; the maneuverable, parabolic action of the horses' ears as they were directed toward some sudden wilderness sound. Now and then, a deer would come out on the road, focus his just-as-maneuverable ears and his eyes on us for a moment, then flip up his tail to show the white "flag," and be gone. The up-and-down rhythmic action of the horses' rumps might almost have lulled one to sleep had there not been a need for continual balance to stay on the high spring seat, despite the seat's five-inch retention safety boards. The ripple of the horses' flank muscles had a kind of biological fascination in itself. There was a physiological marvel in the way the horses raised their tails and eliminated the excretory pellets along the road without the least change of pace. Sparrows took over where the pellets were left. It seemed that the digestive system in much animal life is not thorough. Many undigested oat grains remained for the sparrows to retrieve from the horse pellets.

Something in the leisurely process of movement and periodical rests must have manifested itself strongly to me on these earlier trips and stayed with me, for I still crave a goodly share of leisure and have consistently practiced it at whatever material or monetary sacrifice it incurred. When noon came along the route, the horses were unhitched from the wagon, unbridled, haltered, tied to the side of the wagon, where they ate oats out of feed bags that were strapped to their heads. After consuming the oats, the feed bags were removed, leaving the horses to munch leisurely on hay. Just as leisurely we built a cooking fire and prepared our lunch, oblivious to any travel schedule.

There was a sweet tranquility in it all. The older cousin had a dollar box camera and took pictures of our outfit, but I don't recall that I ever got to see the prints. One can be negligent about priceless treasures.

Toward late afternoon of the second day, we arrived at the shore of a lake in a chain of several lakes, connected by small meandering streams. There, the main camp was set up. One might be amazed today at the cumbersome equipment we carried in the wagon, but at the time it seemed so ideally proper. The tent was pitched, the tarp stretched tightly above it with its own ropes, to serve as a baffle for warding off possible heavy rains. Bedsprings topped with pads were mounted up off the ground on log sections sawed for the purpose. The cook stove was set in place, the pipe projecting through a metal tent-roof thimble; the table and grub-box seats conveniently arranged. Kerosene lanterns were hung on the ends of a cross stick nailed to the supporting tent pole, so that they would cast their glow evenly over the whole tent without shadows. The wagon was drawn up as a manger and protected under the large tarp. We gathered a vast pile of leaves to bed down the horses. All seemed magnificent and impeccably correct to the last item. At the time I would likely not have changed anything, and today as I reflect on it after much study and scientific development of go-light equipment, I would not change anything if, in turning back the crank of time, I could re-create the wilderness flavor of those days.

We fished and hunted enough for our needs. A deer was shot, cut into meal-size chunks, partly roasted in the wood-burning, camp-stove oven, and then packed in an enormous earthern crock. The fat had been fried out and poured hot over the meat. When the fat had firmly set, a cloth was spread over it and covered with about an inch of salt. To use the meat, the salt was lifted off with the cloth, pieces of meat dug out, the fat leveled again with hot fat, the salt and cloth replaced. The meat kept very well throughout the warm weather. A few daily food items were kept cool in a nearby spring.

Scarcely ever did we see anyone on these trips. The lakes were wild, rich in fish. On this particular trip we did meet a small party of Indians who were moving through and had just caught a number of fish which lay flopping about in their canoes. We gave the Indians some flour, lard, salt, and baking powder, sufficient ingredients for bannock. These were the first Indians I had ever seen, and as a youngster I was alive with romantic excitement.

We might attempt to simulate what would happen today under approximately the same geographical conditions. Of course, the wagon would be replaced with the car, the motorized camper, or other such equipment. A portable propane stove would be used, the folding aluminum furniture set up, the boat trailer backed into position, and the boat launched with its outboard motor.

So far, we have made substitutes that might seem in principle roughly equatable with the past. We would travel, in the main, not over narrow country roads but over asphalt highways to a lake, where in crowded camping areas we might observe a dozen boats with outboard motors. If the diversion on arriving at the lake was water skiing, swimming, and a cookout, all might be fulfilled for these pursuits. Obviously the remoteness and seclusion would be gone. The solitude would largely be gone, and just about everything else of wilderness value which the wagon trip possessed down close to the beginning of the century would in distinct contrast be impaired.

Nevertheless, for the wilderness lover there can be a modern solution. You simply go where the country is much the same now as it was early in the century. You aren't, of course, exactly in the wagon-camping category described, because by and large a jeep or a four-wheel-drive vehicle can go where a wagon and horses went. On the other hand, there is a pretty good chance that if you are on a road which only a jeep and not a conventional car can travel, you will have left behind all except the hardy, enterprising, wilderness jeep-driving devotee.

You can go even a step farther than this into the past. You can provide yourself with a highly portable, light camping outfit, a supply of water-free foods, and a canoe or pack horses (see my book *The New Way of the Wilderness*), departing at the end of the crudest road, from a railroad siding, or from a boat that plies wilderness ports. Except for the infrequent, momentary hum of a high-flying plane, you can get so far away from it all that a century time-cranked back from the present could leave you little more apparent isolation.

Much of the hue and cry about the wilderness being gone comes from those who would reach wilderness solitude with a car. One must realize that where one can go with a car without physical exertion, all others can go without exertion, and the chances are that a host of people will be there without exertion when one arrives.

The armchair adventurer thus manages to produce a substantial share of the protest about the disappearing wilderness. He is, nevertheless, the fellow who buys most of the books on the wilderness. I have a humble respect for him, not only because he buys my books too, but because he usually is sincere about his vicarious adventures. There is, of course, a little of the armchair adventurer in all of us. Planning the wilderness venture will always be an important part of both casual and major wilderness travel, and vicariousness can be the prelude that might lead to ultimate actual wilderness experience.

What, one might ask, exactly has happened to the fellow who packed his gear and food supply in a packsack on his back and silently stole away over a rugged wilderness trail? In the earlier part of the century, he could be seen buying supplies around most any wilderness post, or you would find him on a train, or a steamer, bound for some wilderness siding or port. He can be seen today on mountain trails where the spaced Adirondack-type log or stone shelters are provided. There are many people signed and sealed to an asphalt existence who regard the man with a heavy pack, walking the track or road, as a "bindle stiff," the name given a fellow who has his entire earthly possessions in a bundle, and little regard for the establishment; or, if regard he has, then a man of more than common adventurous spirit.

Not too long ago, I was about to board a train headed into

one of Canada's wilderness provinces. At the time, I was carrying a packsack loaded with light camp gear and provisions.
My ticket called for first-class passage. The porter, on seeing
me approach and appraising me as an "undesirable," stepped in
front of me before I could present my reservation, and told
me that I would have to go back to a day coach. Momentarily
perturbed, I took the heavy pack from my back and tossed it
into the porter's arms; he was obliged to brace himself and
catch it or go over backwards. I then gave him my seat number. I think he rather liked the gesture. His race had suffered
enough class distinction to understand that where he and I and
the packsack were concerned, there was neither apartheid nor
pecuniary snobbishness, but actually a rapport. Later we
joked about it.

I have already mentioned that we have become too "comfortized." All of the conveniences at hand today have certainly had their crippling effect upon the natural versatility
and physical capability of too many of us, whatever devices of
mobility have been substituted. In a wilderness youth camp
program which I directed years ago, I couldn't find in a group
of forestry students whom I had hired as counselors, a single
one who could effectively swing an ax. I cannot think of any
of the companions I took along on wilderness canoe voyages
in the early part of the century who could not accomplish this
to a fair degree—some expertly.

That there isn't much of a future today in being able to
swing an ax skillfully, I readily admit. But to see the camping
ability of today, where poor camps in prolonged rain tend to
discourage camping at all, or the cutting short of trips when
an onslaught of bad weather comes on, might suggest that the
effective swinging of an ax needs some revival. Accuracy of
stroke is perhaps the first elementary approach to the practice;
second, some campcraft skill and knowledge; third, the ability

"What has happened to the fellow who backpacked his gear?"

to judge various woods. Some woods are difficult to split beyond practicability, some are poor fuel. Axmanship can be improved by sticking a match; sulphur side up, in the niche of a stump and with one stroke consistently lighting the match with the sharp edge of the ax. The chances are that an aspirant achieving this skill could manage to assemble a reasonably good cold-rain-weather camp, providing, of course, he had some campcraft knowledge to go with his improved axmanship.

There is a strange quirk in the nature of man which allows him a learning modesty about so many things, though scarcely is modesty ever expressed in his ability as a camper. Only in rare instances do you find a man who possesses the fundamentals of campcraft knowledge that will include all-season adverse weather. You might insult a man by speaking disdainfully about his religion or his politics and still survive an onslaught, but suggest by the remotest innuendo to the average camper that he try methods other than his own and you are in trouble. Perhaps this derives from way back in the life of his camping-competent, pristine ancestors, and has survived as a prideful appendage.

When in a cold rain, for example, you come along the shore of a wilderness lake in a canoe and find a camp pitched in a badly selected area, see a frustrated camper blowing desperately to get lively combustion out of soggy or poorly chosen wood, your pity is aroused—but can you do anything about it without offending? If you could, you would tell him that the small dead cedar tree standing on the nearby shore, no matter how long it has been exposed to rain, is as dry a quarter inch on the inside as the desert; that a billet of it cut off and split will kindle a quick fire. He wouldn't even need the birchbark he is using, which hasn't gotten beyond the momentary flash-flame state. You might also suggest to him that the way the weather is progressing on a steady prevailing wind, he had better be on a different shore exposure, where his campfire smoke would be gently carried away from his area instead of

The Adirondack-type shelter.

hanging up like smog. What a temptation it would be to pick up your sharp ax, reestablish his camp on a better site, get up a protective fly to shed the rain, quickly throw up a backlog for a comforting and drying fire—as well as to siphon off the smoke—rake off some glowing embers to one side, and cook a meal. But don't try it. You had better move on graciously, leaving him blowing futilely on his soggy wood. His wife may be with him, and you would by your helpful intrusion shatter his effort to prove to her that he is of heroic fiber.

On a Canadian highway, en route to the North, I once

stopped for lunch at a small public wayside camp area. Occupying one of three tables, a man and woman were struggling with a portable gasoline camp stove. Instead of the usual nice blue flame, a yellow, sooty blaze rose like a bonfire from the burner. He cursed while she stood in awe with the raw, to-be-cooked food. I continued silently with my lunch of sandwiches and a thermos of coffee. When at length I saw no apparent progress in sight with the neighbor's stove, I said, "I've had one of those temperamental contraptions in my 'Carry-All' for years, perhaps I can help you."

"Oh, would you, please?" said the woman.

I picked up the stove, dumped out the raw gas that had accumulated in the manifold from improper priming, and lighted the burners. A nicely regulated blue flame emerged. The woman seemed delighted, but the man walked off a short distance from the table in what seemed to be a peevish sulk. This pair might have had a cold lunch, or none, and stopped at the next town garage for correction of their stove problem, which I am sure should have been the proper solution. Then the man, whom I presumed to be the woman's husband, would not have discovered the truth of the Menckenian observation that "a man's women folk, whatever their outward show of respect for his merit and authority, always regard him secretly as an ass, and with something akin to pity."

I once found a honeybee caught indoors trying to escape through a window. It was just about done for. I dissolved a little sugar in some water and placed a drop where it would have to consume some, if it had life enough left. Slowly it began to revive. I carried it on a sheet of paper to the sunny outdoors. There it quickly revived, *stung me*, and flew away.

Considering the sale of sleeping bags and other camp equipment, there is a fantastic rise in camping interest. But will it be a *now* kind of camping where a great host of unskilled campers will be blowing on soggy or poorly selected wood? Or will it be a renewal of the *then* kind, when most campers could swing an ax; identify good from bad fuel; quickly build a comfortable camp; run a canoe successfully through white-water; pan out a bannock or bake, in a reflector oven, the loaf as tasty as a Sara Lee coffee cake; fix a position with a sextant in a wilderness by an observation on celestial bodies; restring a snowshoe; mend a punctured canoe; know the survival proce-

Bake a tasty loaf in the reflector oven. (An early photo of the author)

dure of an upset canoe (or be so skilled in all kinds of water as to avert an upset); replace a broken paddle with a handmade one, using an ax and crooked knife or a sheath knife; live off the country when supplies peter out or are lost; carry a canoe over a portage without needlessly fighting the load as awkward; pack a load with a tumpline or pack strap and head strap? The list goes on and on.

We might consider some of these components of wilderness life as they existed in the *then* era, and to test the reader's approval, see how many of these can be time-cranked into the *now* era, complements perhaps to modern developments and discoveries that could be pertinent to wilderness life.

A wilderness still remains to be enjoyed. The chances are that we who now live, and those to come, can still discover intrinsic wilderness values. With a new growing consciousness, the wilderness is getting to be regarded less as "a sinful waste," and more as an absolutely essential ecological need for human survival.

It is important that we preserve the basic principles of what "moderns" tend to regard as the outmoded past for comparison with what we think is so potentially valuable for the present. We have the advantage, of course, in past methods that they have been exhaustively tried. We have danger in the future that too many innovations may denigrate wilderness values. The hope, we can assume, lies in junking all but the absolute indispensables in favor of the essential values—a very difficult process that has more to do with empirical sense than caprice or modernization.

4. *Wilderness Happy*

❧

SUFFICIENT YEARS of wilderness living have now been experienced by my wife and me to glean, I think, some kind of advisory perspective on the urban and wilderness environments as they most viably tend to influence us. Both of us earlier were, environmentally, products of metropolitan life. To subject long-urbanized individuals to equally long wilderness living might seem to make of us "laboratory" specimens in determining by contact with both environments which one proves to be what Joseph Wood Krutch has referred to as "The Best of Two Worlds."

One could particularize here with the cliché "best for whom?" I shall be bold enough not to defer to this fallacy, because the human prototype, we have learned by now, is not as self-determining as he thinks, but varies largely in proportion to his physical and mental exposure to a particular, circumstantially compelling environment and its people. He tends to say that he is by choice environmentally and socially more adapted to the city—usually a pseudo-boast. What seems more likely is that he has become addicted to an artificial, obsessive environment from which he is unable, except rarely and then only by desperate effort, to escape. The human animal confined to the city is discovering, though slowly and much to his dismay, that he must of necessity be exposed to natural, wholesome elements in order to develop properly at all. He now lives in a kind of panic, suddenly realizing his urban failure to maintain a viable state, but isn't sure which way he will eventually have to leap to save himself from his rapidly growing, intolerable, environmental hazard.

The self-styled "more-adapted-to-the-city" individual learns that with increasing urban exposure, he degenerates from the fine physical specimen that he most likely was at birth. His mind's wholesomeness is affected as is his body, because by constant urban exposure he seriously impairs the essential natural perspective, perhaps the most vital element in his mental development. He has deceived himself with the notion that the artificiality and mechanization of an urban life are the primary components of intellectual advancement. Technology, the great boon in his early sense of values, he now discovers may tend to destroy him. Man has been extraordinary in many of his accomplishments; but if he is ever to be labeled a fool, it must first be most evident in the ecological province of his thinking, second in his sacrificing health, and third in his disregard for the humanities in favor of an urban obsession with the monetary and material.

There was a time when remoteness from the city meant giving up certain cultural advantages: current news, the theater, opera, symphony, domestic conveniences, electronic communication, luxurious foods—the list is obviously long, depending upon our evaluation of these one-time largely urban components. Radio finally spanned the wide wilderness reaches to bring news and entertainment into isolated regions. Even television has now by its booster system arched over many of these distances. With such communication mediums, along with the pontoon- and ski-equipped plane, the snowmobile and outboard motor, the world's intellectual culture can be made as available for enjoyment in the wilderness as it is in metropolitan centers. The mechanical facility required to bring culture and modernization to remote areas may be what Franklin referred to as paying too much for his jackknife. We can, therefore, afford to be highly discriminating in our choice of items which are purported to civilize.

In a natural environment, with increased leisure and a reposeful tempo of life, there is a greater inclination by circumstance toward the humanities; the profound cultural values obviously have a better chance to be appreciated and assimilated. We can ask in contrast whether in the superimposed smog, turmoil, nerve pressure, and noise of metropolitan life these cultural values have a chance to prosper more than minimally. In fact, it has become evident that urban forces diminish and often entirely prohibit assimilation of man's best cultural efforts, due primarily to the distractions which rob him of the needed solitude.

In wilderness life the culling process with respect to acquaintances, relatives, droppers-in—even those you must at times, for diplomatic reasons and business advantage, show regard for—becomes much less difficult as a qualifying art, much easier to effect without being accused of snobbery. There are in the wilderness, I must admit, some droppers-in—literally, that is, from out of the sky—though circumstance is in one's favor. Pontoon- and ski-equipped planes, as season determines, do set down on the lake in front of our cabin. However, the very process of having to charter a plane to get there, somehow qualifies their arrival as desirable guests. Not that the fat pocketbook needed for plane flight determines acceptability—it certainly does not—but chartered flights tend to give enough importance to the visit to indicate a close friendship, or a meaningful enough call to warrant the plane charter.

Speaking of droppers-in, there is another human element whom we might refer to as "hailers-in." We, here in the wilds of Canada, have somehow acquired in this respect a special affinity for canoe trippers. Our cabin sits on a canoe route sufficiently major in its undertaking to arouse our curiosity as to who in basic character and outlook the voyagers might be. A father and son combination, for example, gives a feeling that a world seemingly torn apart by a generation gap is far more apparent than real in the wilderness environment. A son's bushy haircut with an affected strand hanging over one eye, and a father's "square," closely-cropped haircut might in urban surroundings indicate a generation gap, but on the canoe route the strand over one eye gets brushed aside for improved vision, and unshaven faces bring no distinction because on most canoe trips back through the ages it has become a custom to let beards grow. Earlier it suggested the time-extent of your canoe trip.

We have had a variety of canoe parties stop: craftsmen, university professors, judges and lawyers, doctors and pre-medical students, archeologists, ornithologists, and others; a share of them with their wives as canoe-trip partners. Some reveal, with or without modesty, that they have master's degrees in various studies. The brain-picking my wife and I indulge in on these occasions might suggest that we are being well compensated edifyingly for every cup of coffee we serve to these passing canoeists. But that, I venture to say, has been no cunningly devised plan of ours to expand our mental scope, though expand it does.

We try in some way to reciprocate for such edification. But how do you accomplish this against knowledge imposing as these degrees suggest? Fortunately for all, most people are generous with their knowledge.

With better than a half century of wielding a paddle in wilderness waters and conducting a wilderness program for ten years in organized youth camps, I tend to judge the paddle technique of approaching canoeists through a pair of field glasses, without their being aware of exerting their routine best. Most of them, I have to say, display no "master's degree" in the art. Much of the energy utilized is exerted in trying to keep the canoe on a straight course. A zigzag deviousness is most often in evidence.

The subtlety with which my wife and I approach the opportunity to correct the "paddle-errors-of-their-ways" would do justice to foreign diplomacy. I must say, however, that whatever the skill of these visiting canoeists happens to be, they do not as a rule resist an opportunity for acquiring additional skill on our theory alone. Demonstration is the proof they demand. When in a high wind one manages mastery over the canoe alone with comparative ease, they are properly impressed. We like to observe them as they depart. A share show a heartening improvement, based on demonstrated physical principles long used in wilderness canoe art. Others, my wife

"We have acquired a special affinity for canoe trippers."

He poses listening.   *He gets the message and prepares to drum.*

and I conclude, will never benefit, by a college education, if manual dexterity must be a part of it.

Chronic fishermen from tourist camps seldom come to our shore, although on occasion they want to rid themselves of their catch limit and deposit it for our use so that they can go at fishing again within the law. Those who file off the barbs of hooks in order to throw back uninjured fish, so that fishing can proceed from dawn to dark, are generally, we find, of a breed who have little sustaining qualities to interest the inquiring mind. Invariably they come from a world of industry where material gain on the job and fish pounds in their recreation must be equated for success. Most of them, nevertheless, are presentably good individuals, the success in their lives having apparently been based on the monetary value of "how to win friends and influence people."

The celebrated Susan B. Anthony (a very attractive girl, literature tells us) never married because, as she said, she couldn't find a man with the intellectual qualities she desired.

A PARTRIDGE
GOES THROUGH
THE MATING
RITUAL.

He drums.

*After drumming,
he preens his best
to attract her.*

She lamented the fact that intelligent women married prosaic-minded men just to get a husband. This little episode in the modern emergence of the feminine is called to mind when chronic fishermen bring along their wives on their trips. Wives, by some superior quirk of the feminine mind, seldom can be induced to sit in a boat all day adding to fish pounds, or engage in the asinine pastime I have indicated of catching fish on barbless hooks and throwing them back.

Wives not prone to fish all day, as do their husbands, generally relax in a cabin, perhaps taking the opportunity to read a good book. At times they knit or play solitaire. Now and then, they actually do saunter a short distance into the woods and endeavor to learn something of its secrets. One I talked to pondered the mystery of how the wilderness can possibly perpetuate itself without man's "cultivation."

My wife and I took it upon ourselves on a particular occasion to invite two fishermen's wives and their youngsters for a day of leisurely woodland exploration. Our first discovery was a partridge, which we watched going through its various stages of the mating ritual. Later, we climbed a high crag where with binoculars we could watch the goings and comings of eagles from a nest of young. Toward evening, as we returned to the river where we had left our canoes, a cow moose stood in deep water, then splashed ashore and slowly sauntered into the forest. Thus, we snooped during the day into whatever mysteries of nature the wilds revealed, and saw a great deal that most generally remains obscure to the casual tourist and the chronic fisherman.

Following this jaunt in the woods, we had a visit from the fishermen husbands, who seemed grateful for the diversion we had provided their families. And the fishermen themselves seemed as anxious to enjoy just such a day of exploration as an alternative to fishing all day. Perhaps fishing and hunting guides need to play more diversified, exalted roles, except that most guides have the same fish-pound, acquisition-limit concept of the wilderness as do their patrons.

One of the North Country's most successful wilderness-

"... a cow moose stood in deep water ..."

wise guides has built up a patronage among amateur and professional photographers, where he uses various mating calls
and baiting methods to bring wildlife before the lenses of his
patrons' cameras. Most of this guiding is done during the fly
season when moose are out in the water, and also during the
rutting season when both the bulls and the cows respond to
the mating calls imitated by the guide using a birchbark horn
which brings them boldly and photogenically out on the
waterfront. His photographic patronage, I have observed, is
composed of a far more interesting and sophisticated element
than the hunters who come only to slaughter and reduce to
carrion these magnificent creatures.

With cans of decayed fish entrails or sugar burned to caramel, the guide also manages with these odors to lure many a
bear before the camera—the cans being well concealed from
view in rock crevices to avoid impairing the natural photographic setting. In fact, in the baitings, he has developed a

faculty for good composition as well, choosing such places for wildlife photography as will provide if not pictorial backgrounds, then a complement background that befits the subject. Hunters unsuccessfully seeking his guiding service have invidiously encroached upon his activity with camera fans, hoping for a gun shot. But they do not obtrude very long unless they are immune to scathing insult and willing to take on 235 pounds of brawn, tempered by years of hardening in the bush.

Mere destruction of wildlife can never lead to what the title of this chapter suggests as "wilderness happy." I cite an example. It took nearly a season to bring a crow to eat from our hands. We felt it to be quite an achievement. Perhaps it is a bit farfetched to suggest that a crow can have a captivating personality. We scrounged around for a crow name that would fit his individuality, but came up with nothing more suitable for this ebony-hued creature than just plain Blackie. His dark form would on occasion shadow a window, though most often he waited unobtrusively for his breakfast, giving a deep-throated chuckle when we opened the door. Crows have, I understand, even been taught to utter recognizable words. To that degree Blackie never aspired. Nevertheless we managed a communicative relationship.

One morning quite early during the hunting season an outboard-motor-driven boat drew up near the cabin waterfront, slowed down and stopped. Considering that I was to have a visit, I walked out on the cabin porch. High-powered rifle blasts came within twenty feet of the cabin from the boat of red-coated hunters, the motor being started again amidst the sound of boisterous laughter and a solicitous waving of arms for approval which I did not return. As a result of the shooting, one of Blackie's legs was shattered, hanging in shreds, and in trying to stand, he supported that side by dragging his wing. He seemed to be pleading for my help as I approached him. Another bullet had passed through part of his breast and he was bleeding badly. Soon he lay twitching helplessly, and I knew there was but one recourse for me.

ABOVE: *A log torn open by a bear to get the choice morsels—ants.*

BELOW: *"... to lure a bear before the camera ..."*

How do you feel when you have just mercy-killed a dying friend?

Felix, a red squirrel, has fared better. He scratches on the screen door to arouse us in the morning. His intimacy has reached beyond mere familiarity. He seems to fear no hazard from us. When I am splitting wood, he is apt to arrive from obscurity and leap up on the splitting block. Nor is the raucous noise of a chain saw a deterrent for him. He runs along the saw log and tries to inspect the lethal, moving chain and flying sawdust. I have to keep a finger continually ready on the off switch. But he has his own natural enemies and is ever cautious of them. We scarcely see him when the wind is swaying the overhead boughs. Apparently it simulates too

"Felix, a red squirrel, has fared better."

"Felix has counterparts of some kind at each of our cabin locations." Chipmunk.

closely the sound of rustling hawk or owl wings swooping down for prey. His favorite foods from our supply are roasted peanuts, sunflower seeds, and stale bread, in that order. When peanuts are shelled, he eats them at once. When not shelled, he packs them off for future use. Since he takes the same general route with each peanut, we conclude that he is not burying them at random where he will never find them but is storing them in his larder for the coming winter. On occasion he asserts his "territorial imperative" to other squirrels and imperiously opens up with his machine-gun-like chatter.

Felix hasn't gone wholly domestic. There are times when he seems actually to ignore us. This morning I saw him sitting independently shelling out seeds from the white cedar tree. He is left to his own capable food-gathering resources when we are gone to our several other seasonal residences. The period of estrangement, however, does have a slight alienating effect upon him. On our return he approaches us more cautiously for a day or so, but he is soon scratching on our screen door again, apparently not having suffered any deprivation of nourishment during our absence—still being the same little vibrant, well-fed bundle of rascality that we left. In this delightful independence he reminds me of Vilhjalmur Stefansson and his party, who after living for a year on the game of the

polar ice cap, and being invited on their return to a festive
dinner aboard ship, said: "I am sorry, gentlemen, but we are
not hungry."

Felix has counterparts of some kind at each of our cabin
locations. The process of enticing wild creatures to become
pets gets to be more and more a successfully practiced art.
Perhaps the term "pet" should not properly apply. Gaining
the confidence of wild creatures provides rather a better opportunity to observe them at first hand, and seeing them
around in the adjoining area greatly increases our joy of
wilderness life.

One does not successfully move into the realm of wilderness living without special effort toward gaining such intimacy. Botany is not, we may be sure, studied in detail from
an airplane, nor is a broad objectivity conducive to learning
something about natural phenomena. One needs to move sub-
jectively into the inner circle to hear, to see, to feel, to touch,
to be.

*"Gaining the confidence
of wild creatures . . ."*
Grey squirrel.

Perhaps the entire concept of advantageous wilderness intimacy has its definition in the discovery of what might best be termed the *elemental* approach: the stimulating fragrance of balsam needles crushed in the hand; listening attentively to the mysterious voice of the white-throated sparrow or the hermit thrush in the backwoods; the ever-arresting sound of the loon across a remote wilderness lake; or the howl of a timber wolf at midnight in the far-off winter hills—the list goes on and on of the eternally captivating, often inscrutable impressions.

Just how much truth there ever was in the old adage that ignorance is bliss, I have not been able to determine; nor have I, on the other hand, been able to learn conclusively whether one enjoys an existential comfort of mind in the possession of vast knowledge, be it highly specialized or broadly diversified. What I do believe is that happiness has a much better chance to thrive where the environment offers a natural serenity for gaining knowledge, whether natural or academic. Since my wife and I ran the gamut of metropolitan life for many years, I can hark back for comparison and draw without hesitation the conclusion that we certainly are more wilderness happy than we were urban happy.

Dawn with its many moods breaks ever anew over a wilderness day awakening. The early morning chill often calls for a fire in the Franklin fireplace stove. So, to demonstrate my masculine prowess, I roll out of bed and touch a match to a strip of birchbark and cedar kindling, followed with a few chunks of dry jackpine. A kettle of water is placed on the kitchen stove to heat for coffee. Before I have washed up at the lake front, there are sounds and fragrances emanating from the kitchen which unmistakably suggest that the little lady herself is up and has breakfast under way.

It is a very leisurely breakfast. There is no hint at urgent industry, no bolting of food to catch the 7:40 to work. A flock of loons, or a couple of otter, may swim by to interrupt breakfast and send us sneaking through the shore cover with a telephoto-equipped camera. Then back to a second or third

"*Dawn breaks ever anew over a wilderness day awakening.*"

cup of coffee. Breakfast scarcely ever gets finished without some such diversion, the coffee having to be reheated.

While we indulge in our final cup of coffee, a certain comment on the weather usually is in order. The temperature is recorded, and we note with regularity whether there is a rising or falling barometer. For years we have kidded ourselves about these rising and falling atmospheric pressures; and though we still continue to record the barometric pressures, we have concluded that a barometer is an instrument that foresees no future but merely tells us what kind of weather we are .having at the moment. Were it not for the need of a required barometric pressure reading in my celestial-navigation calculations in deep wilderness travel, the barometer might better be replaced with a pound of bacon.

Some days are so extraordinary, they preempt everything utilitarian we planned for them. There is but one thing to do: load the canoe with essentials, start out, and let the events of the day fall where they may.

There are other days we call "manuscript days" when skies are leaden and seas would argue with every canoe paddle

"A flock of loons may swim by . . ."

stroke. The choice is academic. An open fire down in the studio cabin, a pot of coffee handy, and soon I get lost in ideas, mere reflection, or reading. We have at times, however, headed out in the rain and rough seas because some very interesting things can happen on those days. Moose, bear, and other wildlife more often are on the move during rain. Rainy weather also has that added attraction of being conducive to fabricating some item.

If the sun breaks out by noon, as traditionally as aboard ship, I shoot the sun with a sextant, for here is a subject that comes under the mandate "use it or lose it." The conversation at this juncture of the day runs about like this:

Me: "I think I'll take a sextant shot of the sun."

My wife: "Are you getting hungry?"

". . . start out and let events fall where they may."

"I think I'll take a sextant shot of the sun."

Me: "A little."

My wife: "While you are playing with your *little* instrument, I'll get some lunch on the table."

Naturally there has to be a tie-in between seeking leisure and the privacy of a wilderness retreat. *Retreat* suggests that one is running away from something. In this there is obviously a share of truth, though continued use of the term has given it rather the connotation of *harbor* or *comfortable seclusion.* Perhaps privacy as we practice it becomes a matter of avoiding our inclusion in the "captive industrial grind." Captive to be sure, for how many of the seventy percent of the whole population confined to urban life have not at times had a desire to cut the telephone wires; throw a flat iron through the TV screen, especially where offensive commercials are concerned; adjust ear plugs against low-flying planes and un-muffled motorbikes; deactivate the doorbell; and otherwise shunt off, in one way or another, the thousand and one inroads made on "urban leisure and privacy." I presume it could be said that these encroachments have a nuisance value for the majority, otherwise they would not conveniently place themselves as victims in the center of the urban noise target.

Obviously, a rather wide latitude of difference exists between the noise-seeking, urban-prone, utilitarian citizen's attitude as against that of the artist, the writer, and the humanistic mind seeking an atmosphere of seclusion where ideas can more readily form. To quote Clifton Fadiman, so that I can blame his ego rather than my own for saying it, "Writers, artists, thinkers and heroes are simply more interesting than bankers and railroad presidents. They have more of the leaping stuff of life in them."

However this may be, writers, artists, and thinkers do require less mechanical churning of industry for sustenance of mind than do those in the utilitarian field. Production, if wisely limited, no one doubts is vitally important and essential; yet must one basically give more achievement-prominence to it than to a cow producing milk? I was amazed when a human foot was set down upon the moon, but was it not strictly a mechanical and mathematical achievement? I could be happier had some of the mechanical junk not been left on the moon. Romantically and aesthetically, it suggests too much the junked car lots. Because of the primary mechanistic accomplishment of a moon probe—great mechanistically—interest faded so rapidly its heroes have become indignant and unhappy about the waning popular regard.

Most people living in urban centers are so attuned to mechanical noises, the quiet of the wilderness can be initially distressing. This, of course, is a form of neurosis. Need for accustomed noise can be a craving comparable to a victim's need for narcotics.

If the elemental approach, as I have suggested, is necessary for full enjoyment of the wilderness, some kind of intellectual, aesthetic, or craft program will also be found necessary for its greatest fulfillment.

Focus upon the general world, its politics, its mutations, its culture can be no less a practice in the wilderness than in the city. In fact, there is less a tendency, I believe, to become provincial in one's scope in wilderness life where specialized urban occupations and routines do not dictate. Voice of America radio broadcasts talking to the world reach us here in the wilderness as effectively as they do anywhere else. We are, for example, as concerned over the Czech people being intellectually and physically enslaved by a gang of Kremlin political tyrants as are all other freedom-loving people. A trial of murder-mad morons in Los Angeles, or a freeze of the economy, gets our ear and our evaluation as readily as it does that of the metropolitan resident. Because of the inclination for more natural alternative pursuits, there seems to be less need, in an element of wilderness relaxation, to dwell on or to fret about age-old, apparently insoluble, human conflicts.

The difference between the urban and the wilderness point of view is clearly that in the wilds one tends to receive and regard most news objectively, and perhaps a little more philosophically, by virtue of the vantage point. I say vantage point because much of what seems currently perplexing to people whose lives are empathetically woven into the complex fabric of city life carries less subjective significance for those in the wilderness, beyond an understanding of the problems. All responsible people, of course, need to contribute to human welfare in one way or another. Yet, while the hand of help may seem closer to the problems in the city, it is not necessarily more helpful. The written word or the mailed check can be as effective. The writer in his occupation, though it is practiced in some remote region, can be even more articulate with the problems. I do not necessarily refer to these pages, but to the triumph of literature; the wisdom of the ages, though usually shunned, could have the most effective solutions in resolving man's current problems.

5. The Inner Man Yesterday and Today

❦

NEAR THE beginning of the century Leonidas Hubbard, in his canoe journey with Dillon Wallace and George Elson up the "Terrible Susan" River in Labrador, was caught in the overlapping seasons and died of starvation and exposure. The Franklin party in the Arctic died of starvation and exposure. Reduced metabolism and excessive exposure to cold thus become almost synonymous. Food is heat, and when you don't have food to maintain body heat, you die of exposure.

Comparisons of the wilderness foods available at the beginning of the century with those available now point up some distinct advantages and disadvantages in both eras. If I were to turn back the crank of time to the early part of the century, I would take back with me from the present era a few food items that were direly needed in those days, and reverse the order of time to bring some old ones up to date. At the top of the list in cranking back time would be the modern orange-flavored drink known as Tang. There were, of course, dry powders of the citric acid variety in the earlier days, but where taste and ingredients were concerned, you did a lot better on the side of Vitamin C by drinking the juice from your stewed dried apricots. Apricots are high in the Vitamin C element. You would forego all commercial Vitamin C products if you were in the wilds when rose hips were ripe, or if you found blueberries in season. Rose hips contain the highest Vitamin C content of any fruit.

I would also take back with me into the past the improved instant coffee. (The early instant coffees were abominable.) When today I can get the freshly ground, vacuum-packed coffee, it is, of course, preferred; but on the trail the coffee taste soon adjusts itself to the instant kind, and its convenience and the reduction in weight almost compel its use. I would take back mashed-potato flakes and the precooked instant rice. I would not take back freeze-dried meats, because in those

". . . or if you found blueberries in season."

days meatwise one lived pretty much off the country. Dried
whole milk, not skim or fat-free milk, would be on the take-
back list, especially that kind which is dehydrated by the
latest improved process. And the dry coffee "creams" would
surely be on the take-back list as well, since black coffee to me
is nothing more than what the Indian terms *mukuta muskike-
wapoo*, meaning "black medicine water."

Efforts were, of course, made in the earlier days by various
food companies to dehydrate foods. Some of these foods were
just passable, others bad; or, as one companion claimed, some
tasted like crankcase oil—though here I have to confess that I
have not made an actual taste comparison. Improvement in
dehydrated foods came with time. Those which can be regarded as highly palatable are of comparatively late development; however, dried fruits have always been good, with some
improvement from time to time.

It is possible now to go into the wilderness, and without
refrigeration, capriciously have just about any feast one cares
to prepare and spread. But wisdom dictates that one had better
try ahead of time, at home, anything slated for the wilderness
food budget. There are some items still remaining that might
cause a hungry sled dog to turn up his nose. Then again, many
of the dehydrated products are of such excellence they could
lure the most critical epicure to your wilderness camp fare.

Early-day foods were largely staple items: flour, sugar, salt,
rolled oats, powdered pea meal or pea soup in a stick (*Erbs-
wurst*), white rice, wild rice in season, dried apples, raisins and
apricots, baking powder, yeast and soda for the sourdough
pail, tea and coffee, usually comprised the list. The sourdough
pail—a batter allowed to ferment about three days before take-
off date—consisted of flour, water, yeast, and a spoonful of
sugar. Fermentation continued throughout the trip by daily
replenishing with flour and water. A small amount of soda was
added only to the portion used, converting the sourdough into
a sweetened leavening agent. It was not unusual in the early
days to borrow, from another sourdough friend, a "start"

And, of course, "wild rice in season . . ."

culture for one's own sourdough pail. I came upon a trapper's cabin at one time where the trapper had a sourdough crock that had been going, so I was told, for nine years on the same original cake of yeast. I borrowed a half cup of his sourdough and kept my sourdough pail going on the trail for seven weeks. Sourdough made very tasty pancakes and bannock. It contributed, without waiting on each individual baking, to that quality so desirable in fresh yeast bread. Where bannock was made with baking powder as the sole leavening agent and used over a period of several days or more, it created an uncomfortable condition of excessive intestinal gas.

There was a pretty good chance that the first meal on a trip would be fish. Also, before a day or two had passed, fresh meat of some kind was usually procured—perhaps duck, partridge, or rabbit. As the trip progressed, a deer or caribou was shot and a substantial share of it converted to pemmican or jerky. If one came upon Indians, one could, from time to time, trade some tea or flour for a generous meat supply. Jerky was made by cutting meat, as fat-free as possible, into long narrow strips and drying these strips in the sun on a rack made from poles. A small fire was kept going under the meat, not near enough to cook it, but only to provide enough smoke to keep off flies and to give the meat a slightly smoke-cured taste. Pemmican was made by pounding the dry jerky strips on a stump until flaked, then the fat from the animal was rendered and poured hot into the meat flakes. The animal hide was sewed into bags and the pemmican, while still soft, put into these skin bags, which were then closed. No salt was used, since this would have drawn moisture and spoiled the pemmican.

The reflector oven, known rather early, became a popular utensil and is used today by some wilderness travelers. But around the early part of the century (and much earlier), the traditional bannock baked by reflection in a frying pan supplied the breadstuff. Before metal pans were available, Southwest Indians ground corn into flour with hand millstones and baked the loaf by reflected heat on a flat rock, although in the pueblo and permanent camps the *horno*, or adobe oven, was used. Later through the West came the sixteen-quart iron kettle known as a Dutch oven. It still has great merit in wrangler cookout camps, and I highly recommend it for packhorse trips.

While the reflector oven is an extraordinarily fine utensil, it is, even when folded, a bulky, not essential, item in the equipment. The highly mobile wilderness traveler, especially if he had his complete equipment and food supply in a packsack on his back, showed disdain for the reflector oven and became an expert with the bannock pan. This whole process is described at greater length in previous publications of mine, to which the reader can refer for all his needs. The important thing is that the frypan-like utensil should have rather straight sides. Staple, plain bread was generally the standard bannock type, but there came a need now and then for a sublimated loaf, one

"Later through the West came the sixteen-quart Dutch oven."

The traditional bannock pan.

loaded with raisins, milk powder, sugar, stewed apples or apricots, to make it a kind of coffee cake. With coffee or tea it heightened spirits on a rainy-day delay in camp. There is something inspirational about freshly baked bread. I believe that many women would have lessened the task of the divorce courts had they welcomed their husbands at the end of the work day with the smell of freshly baked bread.

What stand out, in comparing the early provision list with that of today, are the staple items as against the processed items in the two lists. The sack of flour that topped the list was basic. With its complement ingredients it represented what today is a long list of processed, packaged items, such as pancake flour, wrapped and sliced bakery bread, crackers, noodles, biscuit mixes, etc. Application of this basic staple concept in early times applied pretty much to the entire provision list, and a desired economy could bring it back into modern use.

Though the market began rather early to have prepared items on the shelves, such as pancake flour, the bygone wilderness traveler was not at a loss. He made his own mixes ahead of time so that he need only add water to come up with, say, a pancake batter, a biscuit mix, or whatever he chose.

In fact, the first mix that I saw was made by some Cree Indians in a Hudson's Bay Company Post. The factor, a rather ingenious young Scotchman, had made what he called a "mixing tumbler"—a barrel mounted on a stand in such a way that when revolved it would up-end. You dumped all of the dry ingredients, including softened shortening, into one end of the barrel, closed it with a flat wooden bolted-on slide, and slowly turned a crank, the up-ending of the barrel at every turn mixing the ingredients. The Indians were pleased with the arrangement and laughed hilariously as they turned the crank. The tumbler stood high, so that the mixed ingredients were easily dumped into the original flour sack, hung beneath the tumbler opening. When the Indians reached camp they simply pushed a fist into the flour mixture, poured some water into the depression, stirred the water momentarily with a stick until a wad of dough formed, picked out the wad, worked it a bit between the hands and flattened it out in the bannock pan to bake. This barrel mix was, of course, a baking powder process. The sourdough leavening agent could not be so treated but had to be mixed with other ingredients on the trail. I have already alluded to the use of baking powder as unwise if prolonged. The sourdough process, on the other hand, provided a very healthful leavening agent, giving certain vitamins as well as assisting digestion.

The processing of modern-day foods requiring harmful preservatives, as we all know, has embattled consumer, processor, and the government. This could be one reason, besides economy, for starting out on the trail even today with staple products. The difference in cost between staples and the processed items that result in the same end products is about five to one in favor of the staples.

Today in a wilderness cabin one tends to live similarly, foodwise, as one does in the city. If, for example, there isn't fresh cream for the coffee in the wilderness, then there is the powdered item called Coffee Mate, or similar products which have almost as universally found their way onto many city tables. Somehow you can't freeze coffee cream and thaw it out without its curdling in the coffee; but you can freeze homogenized milk, thaw it, give it a few shakes and it reconstitutes perfectly—an advantage my wife and I have added in remote cabin living. Frozen hard at the start, it survives spoiling, if insulated, by most any means of transportation to cabin living.

If you have so capricious a taste that you cannot drink your coffee without fresh cream and require other perishables, and possess an unlimited budget, there is always the plane. The most extravagant example of this I have known was the delivery of fresh food by plane every week to a cabin camp almost two hundred miles from a supply. The weekly food cost for the small family was nominal, the transportation cost exorbi-

tant by common standards. But what does it matter to those
who never suffer austerity?

The luxury of modern-day foods, as compared to the staples of earlier periods, calls up a vast change and whole new
outlook on human existence. There is an old saying: "If you
have acquired knowledge you are compelled to live with it."
One might add to this: "Ignorance is bliss." What I am trying
to point out is that when life was a lot less complex, less
encumbered with countless processed food items and innumerable gadgets, the concern for economic security weighed
less heavily. For the wilderness resident this was especially
true.

In modern living one no longer thinks in terms of grubstakes. Today a grubstake would more likely be regarded as
enough money to carry one through an extravagant period. In
the early days one thought of a grubstake as just that—*provisions*, a supply of staples that would carry one through, say, a
winter. Earlier, one arrived in the wilderness with such items
as varying-size sacks of flour, rice, beans, split peas, salt, sugar,
rolled oats, unground green or roasted coffee beans, tea, caddies of dried fruit, slabs of bacon, whole hams, a small wooden
tub of butter, and lard in covered metal pails. Canned and
processed foods thus did not enter into the grubstake to mul-
tiply, as they do today, the cost of subsistence a number of
times.

Just how the average housewife or modern recreationalist
would handle such staples, I can only conjecture. I haven't the
least doubt, however, that when either of them became hungry, necessity and some basic recipes would wake up the
mother of invention. And further, the imaginative good cook
of today could, no doubt, produce from staples a table fit for
the most discriminating taste.

The comparison I like to make is that the concept of gaining long leisure periods by using staple food grubstakes seems
to have become almost nonexistent in the modern world.
People are occupationally trading many priceless hours of life,

year in and year out, to maintain costly processed food budgets, when the economy of staple foods could buy back some of the leisure they desire. The increase of time needed to prepare staple foods over processed foods is a small investment compared to the on-the-job time confinement needed to buy the processed, drug-preserved foods. Perhaps Julia Child's classic cookery on TV will point up the need to use staple ingredients for the preparation of superior foods.

With average good fortune we tend to gather a certain amount of affluence later in life, of course, so that the processed foods and "luxurious" gadgets come rather easily when, as one man put it, they come too late for good digestion and capable utility.

I often wonder what I would have done had I been ushered into the world as a young man facing extravagant methods and processes on the same austere basis that I faced them near the early part of the century. At that time, with a cabin stocked for the winter with sacks, caddies, and small tubs of staple foods, along with a deer, moose, or caribou hung in the meat cache, I felt rich and secure. Or, perhaps, I did not think about the hazard of insecurity at all, which had much to do with this staple food approach. Leisure time I have always regarded as a necessity too valuable to be easily negotiable.

6. Thoreau–An Afflatus

ANY reflection upon the natural scene of past years cannot fail to consider Henry David Thoreau and his growing influence upon our way of life. Apparently it has come—a natural afflatus; that is, recognition, finally, of the overmastering knowledge that is Thoreau, and what he stood for.

What essentially did he stand for? Perhaps it can best be described as a mode of socially and ecologically sound procedure—almost the reverse of the social and industrial stress that occupies the world today. We might observe what we have been doing badly to perpetuate our personal welfare, then read Thoreau to get what, more elementally, we might better have pursued—not in imitation of him, but symbolically of his attitude and tempo of life—that would permit us to be happier creatures and give us a greater hope of ecological survival.

I suppose that individually we see great wisdom in the writings of others which we can equate with our own personal point of view, but Thoreau's advice has become a basic and inescapably wise pronouncement. In principle, early in life I practiced on my own what many years later, in essence, I discovered in more comprehensive form in the writings of Thoreau.

The works of Thoreau have flowed in translation to just about every part of the world. To say this has been chiefly the result of his literary achievement alone, rather than intrinsically of the lessons contained in his writings, would be like indulging only in the dessert course of a pretentious epicurean spread. The main course of his writings has revealed at last the cardinal mistakes of our industrial obsessionism. He states his case against it without compunction, for he was as sure as most are now becoming that even then in the industrial madness:

> It is a fool's life, as they will find before they get to the end of it, if not before.

One need not theorize alone on the validity of such advice. I pose an example: At Marine on St. Croix, Minnesota, on the picturesque bank of the St. Croix River, a half hour's drive from a metropolitan center, my wife carries on her domestic program in a modern, button-pressing home for about five months of the year. Alternately, just as many months are spent in wilderness cabins and on the trail, where *running water* becomes such only if you care to run rather than walk with a bucket from the lake or spring.

Handicap?

Adjustment to this kind of frontier life becomes incredibly routine and as natural for her as for me. Thoreau in this respect suggests:

> It would be to some advantage to live a primitive and frontier life, though in the midst of an outward civilization, if only to learn what are the gross necessities of life and what methods have been taken to obtain them. . . .

"... *frontier life becomes as natural for her as for me.*"

In the numerous reviews of Thoreau's writings one sees a pedantic clique jumping eagerly on such a text, asking apparently in wide-eyed consternation: "Are you suggesting that we revert to the primitive and give up all our modern improvements?" In this type of response we have seen failure to understand essentially either the wisdom of Thoreau or the current social and environmental problems. Thoreau suggested metaphorically that you "keep your accounts on your thumbnail." We might even believe that this has some advantage over the digital computer, if we are to judge the merits of what industry has done to a natural world, and especially what it has done to humanistic man. If "the mass of men lead lives of quiet desperation" in industrial strife, as Thoreau stated even in 1854, we can be sure that he would wince at the thought of man today becoming so urbanized as to be little more than a small cog in a vast machine. More particularly we might say that man has become a cog in a machine within a machine, for his employment within the mechanism of industry within the metropolitan artifice, and alternatively within the home which has become a machine, removes him as far as possible from the viable, natural environment indispensable to his well-being. This becomes true no matter how we are compelled by circumstance to condone industry and modernization.

It should not be considered presumptuous to suggest that "civilization" to be realized ought to civilize. To civilize is to educate, refine, and humanize, if basic definitions mean anything. To educate is obviously to develop and cultivate mentally and morally. To presume that this can be done by packing ourselves within the confines of an untenable urban area, where not a breath of fresh air is drawn and our drinking water is the chemically treated effluent of a sewer-ridden river, is certainly a lamentable presumption of civilizing. If to educate is also to refine and humanize, obviously it must imply an environment in which refinement and humanity can develop and thrive. When competitive enterprise, for example, is not satisfied with extolling the virtues of its own product, but must vindictively and avariciously spend vast advertising fortunes deriding the products of others, refinement and humanization are scarcely civilization's boast.

Certainly the most neglected aspect of the much-needed civilizing process is repose, a concept on which Thoreau dwelt at length:

> Why should we live with such hurry and waste of life? We are determined to be starved before we are hungry. Men say that a stitch in time saves nine, and so they take a thousand stitches today to save nine tomorrow.

Congress has been provoked into doing something, if only rhetorically, about restoring the environment. They tell us it will take billions—a great many billions. Thoreau warned us, Mark Twain warned us, Stewart Udall warned us. The untold billions now to be exacted from the populace to restore the natural environment need never have had to be spent had we heeded the Thoreaus, or the sane, less celebrated, subsequent minority who pleaded, and to this day plead, in vain.

"Simplify, simplify," said Thoreau. "Complicate, complicate," suggests the industrial world. And when complication causes great perplexity, industry applies more complication to overcome the earlier complication. Consider for a moment the modern-day pertinence of Thoreau's remark:

When we are unhurried and wise, we perceive that only worthy things have any permanent and absolute existence.

But we have not been unhurried and wise. We have been hurried and crassly foolish in dealing with man and his environment, especially where the noblest of human values are concerned. Consider the "permanence" and "absolutes" of planned obsolescence, the impermanence of most plastics, and the minimal regard for the humanities.

Says Thoreau: "If the engine whistles, let it whistle until it is hoarse for its pains." We have on this score been utilitarian rather than humanistic. "If the bell rings," he continues, "why should we run?" This seems less metaphoric than actual. But if one cannot understand metaphor, one cannot understand Thoreau. If one cannot understand implication, one should not read Thoreau. On the other hand, if man is to survive at all, he had better give serious heed to both the Thoreaus of yesterday and their counterparts of today.

Thoreau's reviewers and critics have been many. He has been profoundly understood and obtusely misunderstood. One English professor derided Thoreau for not having been hermit purist enough to remain continuously at the Walden cabin during the period of his experiment. This critic, apparently devoid of rationality, further derided him for not preparing all of his own meals, considering Thoreau's experiment a failure because he accepted an occasional dinner invitation. Thoreau's experiment was obviously intended to be pleasurable and profound, not the masochistic wearing of a crown of thorns.

The vituperation that comes from the establishment's most avid proponents for continuing the industrial nightmare at its present tempo is too apparent to require examples. Pedantic nit-pickers of the classic Thoreau offer the best examples of how the human caged animal—satisfied with the food and shelter he gets from his captors—fails to grasp the liberating values which Thoreau depicted. These values, he made clear, should be the rightful heritage and current advantage of everyone.

Thoreau has been, and will continue to be, a thorn in the side of industrial obsessionism that has ignored preservation of the world. Reckless ravage of our natural and human resources for profit finds no condonation in the pages of a publication such as *Walden*. On this point, Thoreau says:

> The finest qualities of our nature, like the bloom on fruits, can be preserved only by the most delicate handling.

The best in man, it seems, has so far largely been handled with ugly crate hooks.

Here on the shores of Marchington Lake, though in a cabin far more pretentious than what Thoreau constructed with his own hands—one, however, we too built with our own hands —we find an intimate kinship with his general outlook on life and in essence what some of his thoughts might have been on the shore of Walden Pond. But the elemental nature of this concept has perhaps been more fully realized by us in some less pretentious shelters.

We dare not, of course, compare costs with him. His total expenditure for cabin materials was $28.12½. Yet, on the whole we did not fare much worse where old and new costs are to be computed and compared. We bid $100 on an abandoned wilderness schoolhouse and got it, salvaging thousands of feet of well-seasoned lumber, spacious windows, heavy doors, and a hardwood floor. We had the further advantage

"... a cabin we,
too, built with
our own hands ..."

". . . some less pretentious shelters."

that every board had been saturated with scholarly teaching, while Thoreau for $4.25 bought the residence of an Irishman, James Collins, deploring:

> It was dark, and had a dirt floor for the most part, dank, clammy, and aguish. . . .

What culture Thoreau failed to find in his cabin-material salvage in the Irishman's hut, he made up in the building of his own cabin—an edifice of literature which grows in intellectual prominence with each succeeding era.

If my wife and I should ever be worthy of a documented criticism, I am afraid that we will fare badly with the professorial, master's-degree-in-English critic, since we, like Thoreau, are not impeccable wilderness purists. There are months when we are not in the North American wilderness. As Thoreau sinned by accepting dinner invitations, so do we sin dreadfully. We might even on occasion indulge in such distressing breaches of wilderness ethics as dining in America's best hotels. In *Walden* on "Economy," Thoreau writes:

> When I wrote the following pages, or rather the bulk of them, I lived alone in the woods, a mile from any neighbor, in a house which I had built myself, on the shore of Walden Pond, in Concord, Massachusetts, and earned my living by the labor of my hands only. I lived there two years and two months. At present I am a sojourner in civilized life again.

And so are we disposed, though one is tempted at times in the present era to put quotation marks around the term *civilized*.

7. *Hands and Feet Upon the Wilderness*

Ɛ

SOMEWHERE I heard repeated a conversation between a manicurist and a new customer, wherein the manicurist exclaimed: "What has Madam done with her hands?" "I used them" was the reply.

Much has been written technically about reflex action, about habit, the function of involuntary and voluntary muscles, though such texts scarcely ever get removed from scientific treatment and brought down to the nub of things for the average of us. In fact, the tendency through history has been to give only secondary credence to manual dexterity—except in sports. Earlier, one heard the expression "brains over brawn." It was a boast. Those who used their hands to make a living gained little prestige. Lily-white hands—which probably also meant a white liver—suggested that the owner had transcended "vulgar labor." Manual skill, a category in society that rose a phase above common labor, did not yet exalt the manually skilled individual. "Brains over brawn," as a social manifestation, dies hard.

Much effort to deride manual sense has come defensively from physically clumsy people. A sharp tool in their hands can possess self-destructive potential, though the individual might possess normal intelligence. Some people claim that they are not very capable with their hands, which ostensibly is said to imply that they have capable minds.

A medical student who came to visit and watch me build a cabin gave the implied boast, "I am not very good with my hands."

"That's unfortunate," I said, "but I wouldn't worry about it." Knowing that he wanted to be a surgeon and that he had an interest in golf, I continued: "You can still be a good internal medicine man without having to practice surgery, and golf isn't everything." I found from his reaction that my answer was not conducive toward winning a friend and influencing kindly a construction spectator.

A common fallacy exists that men of genius cannot satisfactorily perform such simple functions as tying a necktie. Contrarily, I have found that most of them usually master ordinary functions of life much better than the average man.

Once we begin to place people in special categories regarding their intellectual and manual skill we, of course, compound our confusion. I have met superior athletes who couldn't give you an intelligent answer on any subject, even athletics; and I have met athletes who have far greater potentials than being compelled solely to flex their muscles for profit. If an individual is so awkward that he stumbles over his own shadow, he can still be useful, but he had better leave most manual functions, no matter where he is, to the fellow whose hands and feet have some kind of coordination.

Where life in the wilderness is concerned, he would, of course, live in continual jeopardy. If he loves the wilds and can afford it, he might better place himself in the custody of an experienced wilderness guide.

A wilderness neighbor of ours who seems to have a general fondness for people gave up inviting friends from the city, particularly for the reason that too many were accident prone.

On this Precambrian rock shore, for example, there is a rise and fall of water that deposits slippery microscopic vegetation below the high watermark. Yet, the warning the novitiate gets is of no avail, so that far too often one finds oneself employing a plane to fly out a broken-arm case to the hospital. Others cut their feet with axes, while still others upset canoes—most often at the shore, strange as this might seem, though not strange in principle when one considers that the bow of a canoe resting on shore provides a hazardous canoe-tipping fulcrum.

While some of these accidents might seem to be removed from manual sense, they generally are not. What is involved here is an understanding of simple physical law, an important

"*. . . roaring whitewater rapids of a wilderness river . . .*"

complement to manual processes anywhere. Manual sense appears to be an instinctive faculty of those who possess it rather than something acquired, though varying degrees of development are possible. As a youngster playing football, I saw one of my teammates about to kick the ball while standing on a small area of ice. Several of us shouted, "Don't!" but too late. His feet, as he kicked the ball, went up, his head down, and he died an hour later from a fractured skull. The inertial principle here will be obvious.

People who are brought up performing manual chores generally know what will happen in the process of handling wilderness equipment. Can it be that Indians down through the ages, traveling over rugged terrain, have developed superior footing? The late author Stewart Edward White noted that in the wilderness each step is of a different length, each of a different height, each of a different quality. As one tries to follow a woods Indian through the wilderness, it soon becomes evident that the expediency of the Indian's pace exceeds one's own. If one tends to doubt this, watch the steelwork of a New York skyscraper going up: it will be Indians to a large extent who are doing the work. For an answer to why Indians should preferably be chosen, I talked to a building construction engineer. He said, "They are surefooted as hell."

One pair of capable hands can take you by canoe through the roaring whitewater rapids of a wilderness river and bring you safely into the placid waters below, or ride out a sea with a canoe that might swamp a craft of "mightier beam." Or, a pair of such hands could hew a timber so square and true, that were it not for the surface texture difference, you would suspect from the symmetry of the timber that it had come from the aligned blade of a sawmill. I like to think about the hands of a great surgeon, as well, where manual sense is coupled with prodigious knowledge. A famous surgeon once told me that a very skillful mechanic might have developed into a competent surgeon, had the turn of events been such in the initial period of choice.

I get a number of letters from those who would take up life in the wilderness. "Do you think that I"—and they usually offer meager qualifications—"can manage the various tasks pertinent to a wilderness life?" One's empathy and admiration is so wholeheartedly with those who want to do so, that the serious, helpful reply is difficult to dredge up. In these instances one needs to be more concerned, I think, with the potential of the correspondent's common manual capabilities than with his limited wilderness experience. From a strictly practical viewpoint, one might rather have as a partner on a long canoe or sled journey a man who, though he had no wilderness experience at all, could, for example, consistently hit a ball with a bat, than a man with a master's degree in physics who had little manual sense.

The argument is often entered as to what qualities are possessed by the most competent woodsman. One might, of course, ask here: "What is meant by a competent woodsman?" A prosaic definition of a woodsman could merely be the man who is most capable of carrying on successfully and fruitfully the necessary utilitarian functions of wilderness life. Whatever attributes and accomplishments of manual sense and theoretical knowledge are to be considered, the greater handicap exists where one is obliged to maintain wilderness life on a minimal manual sense and a maximal theoretical knowledge, rather than the reverse of these.

In an urban environment, contrary to that of the wilderness, there need be little focus, except in the trades, on the ability of the layman to perform manual tasks, though some whose work is sedentary do, as exceptions, keep up with their own hands the repair of their premises, and in conjunction have commendable manual hobbies. However, in the city the trades can be called in to do the job at a price. In the wilderness you do not call, you *do*. When the outboard motor, the chain saw, or any other unit quits, you had best learn why and proceed to correct it yourself. If a giant tree falls on your cabin, you remove it yourself and repair the roof. If you are not the proverbial jack-of-all-trades, you need to possess the resourcefulness at least to get current living back on the track, or invade enough trade prerogatives to get wilderness appliances working again.

When our propane gas refrigerator gave a perfectly normal flame but wouldn't "refrig," the extent of our self-vaunted resourcefulness finally petered out. There was an alternative, of course; we could fly out the unit on a chartered plane for service, and back again, at a cost of about a hundred dollars for transportation alone. The only other recourse was to communicate some way with a distant propane service station and get elaborate instructions. In this communication I expected to acquire considerable technical information in order to meet the challenge of dismantling, repairing, and reassembling the refrigerator. When I received the serviceman's instructions I

"What is meant by a competent woodsman?"

thought he had indulged in too much of Canada's Scotch whisky.

"Stand it on its head for eight hours," he said. "Then set it upright for eight hours more before you light it again."

Well, I thought, it seems to be an insane idea; but who am I to argue with modern science? We did set it on its head with the aid of two husky local Indians. At first they argued rather vehemently that it had not been designed to run that way. The shelves would fall off their supports, they said; and besides, you couldn't get the legs off to put them on the other end.

But I said, "Just for eight hours."

The next day I asked them to help me set it back on its legs. They seemed pleased that I had changed my mind about the whole business. From what little of the Cree tongue I knew, I was able to grasp that they felt I had apparently regained my senses.

Eight hours later we lit the refrigerator. It has worked well ever since. The inversion was needed to clear up an air block in the refrigerant. I suggested to my wife that should we be taken ill, we might resort to yoga and stand on our heads for a spell.

When earlier we tried to get a carpenter and his helper to rough in the main cabin, we couldn't get any of them to live in a tent, sleep on cots, and cook their meals on a gasoline stove. The day of the pioneer spirit, apparently, had gone into limbo with the advent of unions and power saws. If we could supply them with prepared meals and lodging in the fishing camp two miles away, and also provide someone to transport them by boat and motor, morning and evening, they said, they would take the job. We added it up: union wages, plus lodging and meals at resort prices, plus boat transportation. "I'm sorry," I said, "I'll have to make other plans." Their response would not look good in print.

Their general attitude became a challenge for us. My wife and I got out the carpenter tools. By the following day we had a sub-floor deck laid on the previously poured concrete footings and a tent pitched on the deck—the tent heated in the fifty-degree temperature of evening with a gasoline lantern. There were no union hours. We worked from dawn to dark. An Indian friend of ours came by occasionally and sometimes, without stopping, threw some freshly caught fish up on the rocks. On one occasion he praised our progress and said, "You can't eat fish all the time," taking from his pack two dressed partridge.

A day came when the tent was taken down because we had a roof over our heads and the cabin walls roughly closed in with windows and doors. Only the monotonous job of putting on the siding and inside paneling remained. That, we concluded, we would do leisurely—a little at a time between recreation and other things.

But something happened in the immediate, outside, industrial and social world that changed our plans. The railroad division-point had been moved, leaving the area of the old division-point in a kind of economic depression. Carpenter jobs had become scarce, work dwindling until the pride which demanded resort subsistence and motorized transportation had diminished to the point where the carpenters were now willing to sleep in a tent and do their own cooking. They would, they said, build our cabin for us on the terms we required. Our answer was brief, "We are living in it." Necessity has proved at times to be more than the mother of invention.

A local trapper skilled with woodworking tools made a bid for the job of putting on the siding and the inside paneling and laying the hardwood floor, to relieve us of the monotony of these jobs. He made no luxurious subsistence demands. Every morning at 7:30 his canoe would reach our shore regardless of weather. When it rained he would put on inside paneling or lay flooring; between rains he would put on siding. Self-driven, he put in every minute sedulously cutting and fitting. His canoe trip in the cold rain seemed to me to call for a warming cup of coffee, but only when I facetiously reminded him that "the boss will never know you relaxed now and then" did he partake in coffee breaks and the occasional round of conversation.

Mechanization and efficiency-driven employment have replaced the leisurely craftsman. For less than fifteen minutes of a craftsman's minimal wages, one can now buy a hickory, machine-made, ax handle. But the "song" is not in it. And, no doubt, one would be a fool to recommend as a point of economy that an ax handle be crafted by hand. So, today I, too, buy ax handles, going through the dealer's stock for those which will hang true on the blade, and where the wood *grain* is not, as Robert Frost has charmingly indicated in his classic lines:

> Across the handle's long drawn serpentine,
> Like the two strokes across a dollar sign.

The average, complete, good ax of drop-forged steel and hickory handle costs less than ten dollars today. Yet, let us consider for a moment value versus price. A hand-forged ax blade with a handmade handle was recently sold at an antique auction for one hundred and thirty-five dollars. It is now suspended below an original Philip Goodwin painting of a North Country subject over the fireplace in a rather pretentious though picturesque cabin on the bank of the St. Lawrence River.

In this ax—an extraordinary piece of handwork—there *is* a song. It was made by an unknown craftsman in the pioneer days of American settlement.

In my early wilderness days I recall how we made and stored the spare ax handle, should the original handle break. A few billets of shell-bark hickory wood were hand-ripped from a straight-grained, second-growth tree, peeled and allowed to season for a year or so. As in the aging of wine, the seasoning of billets had to be projected well into future need. On occasion, one could buy the seasoned billets, or even the handmade, finished handles. But most often the custom was to make the handle oneself. A skilled craftsman could rough out the handle with a sharp ax in an hour or so, though the actual finishing of the handle with rasp and sandpaper was a job for more leisurely hours. A hickory billet or roughed-out handle might even be left hanging in the chimney corner back of the stove for a few additional weeks to see if any grain stresses would develop that might possibly give the handle an ultimate warp. As the rasp and sandpaper were used to finally shape it up, one would see the maker sighting along the helve now and then to be sure that it was truing up. One observed a confident gripping of the handle for proper feel and a nod of approval as it successfully shaped up.

Not long ago I went through a woodworking plant where ax handles and canoe paddles were being made by machinery. They dropped out of automatic wood lathes and were surface-finished in great profusion amidst the speed of screaming machines. The owner brought me into his office to a highly appointed lounge with soundproofed walls, thick rugs, deeply upholstered chairs, and a fireplace, where we were insulated from the adjacent raucous industry. Displayed in a walnut-framed glass case, built into the pine-paneled wall, was an ax handle. "That handle," said my host, as he served coffee to me, "was the last commercial handle my grandfather made by hand before he installed a wood lathe." My host unlocked the case so that I might examine the select hickory grain, get the feel of it, and sight along its "long drawn serpentine" for perfection of balance. Absent in the grain were "the two strokes across a dollar sign."

"You wouldn't replace it with a handle from your present factory?" I asked with a smile. He pressed the intercom button and instructed someone to bundle up two select hickory ax handles and two ash canoe paddles. "Take these with you," he said, "they aren't much, but that's all that I can offer you that is left of a family tradition." As I later entered my car with the complimentary handles and paddles, I could hear the high-decibel scream of automatic wood lathes diminishing behind me. For several miles the glass-encased, handmade ax handle whose grain flowed with its "serpentine" curve returned nostalgically to mind like a magnificent ghost image of perfection out of the past.

Today when planned obsolescence is in high priority, the

Eskimo-crafted items.

individual who will try his hand at manual skill can glean from life a great many lost values. Wilderness life held without a manual grip on it is culturally weak. The ability, for example, to tie perfectly simulated trout flies and construct a fine Toncan bamboo flyrod is an achievement so elementally desirable and satisfying, that no highly affluent expenditure for the finest commercial equipment in the world could offer comparable values. There was a time when items could be custommade commercially, but no amount of inducement in this modern day seems alluring enough to pull the supercraftsman away from the mechanized production center.

The stereotyped form dominates for production's sake, which economically is helpful. But let us not abandon the classic art form that endures as the individualistic expression, lest we lose the true values of life. A computer can never paint the masterpiece.

Some items are beyond purchase. In my book *Paradise Below Zero* I have offered to give sources for those winter wilderness items which the reader fails to find in the open market. Commercial mukluks, moccasins, and mittens for the winter wilderness traveler are tragically inadequate. Skins smoke-tanned by Indians and Eskimos, crafted into native-patterned footwear and mittens, are required to make sub-zero wilderness living and travel highly functional. It pains me that I cannot suggest ample sources for such items to my readers. Fine smoke-tanned skins today are quite scarce, except in remote wilderness areas. To hope for acquisition of such items through correspondence has proved virtually impossible. The amicable, personal contact is needed. Factory-tanned skins are worthless for this purpose because the smooth grain is not removed, and when left on mukluks, moccasins, or mittens only risks perspiration condensation, with consequent danger of frozen hands and feet.

Much wilderness equipment thus finds the only solution in personally conceived patterns and self-made, individually fitted items. Many fine commercial items can be purchased, but most of them have to be restyled to be highly practical. Most sheath knives and axes have to be reground for edge taper to make them cut properly. Parkas and sleeping bags need to be altered—if nothing more than getting rid of abominable zippers and replacing them with proper snap or button closures that work.

The question: "Why don't you suggest such changes to manufacturers?" I have. Usually suggestions only offend, and scarcely ever does a firm consider redesign once an item is on the market, due to the high cost of conversion. Most manufacturers have little, or no, practical field knowledge. Besides, many items would not appeal to the popular trade if they were given the most practical design, strange as this may seem. Some manufacturers have on rare occasions deferred to suggestions from people in the field and made items that are "right." But the right item does not sell nearly as well as the popularly accepted, impractical one. For example: The largest aluminum canoe manufacturer has a canoe made in the Prospector design. It is an excellent craft and in competent hands will outride most any sea and whitewater. The firm also makes an aluminum canoe that comparably is a poor design. Nevertheless, it outsells their properly designed canoes because the ends arc up in rather sensuous, though valueless, "attractive" curves. In the Prospector model the metal used in these useless upturns has been taken away and the gunwale curve redesigned, leaving the canoe the same weight but absorbing the upturn material so that it is not bizarre in design, yet highly functional in value. This improved canoe sells mainly to the experienced canoe voyager.

There is some improvement today in commercial items of wilderness equipment, though most exploration-party equipment, at least, has to be custom-made or remodeled. Earlier, it was impossible for explorers to find proper commercial clothing, and their only solution lay in adopting native Eskimo- and Indian-made items.

Thus, the individual's skillful hands need to be applied upon the wilderness. This discussion might end on the following note, with which most intelligent people will agree: In a world of insecurity, of planned obsolescence, of ephemeral plastics and other impermanency, the individual who can reach back into a more stable world, or ahead if you prefer, and come up with genuine, durable items, methods, and principles—life, to that individual, will have far greater values and pleasure.

High-speed production is not likely to gain nearly the chance for happiness that fine, durably crafted items made at a leisurely pace offer. Japan has discovered the value of shipping abroad only quality products. Man may walk to happiness and get there sooner than if he tried to reach it with infinite speed.

8. *Women in the Wilderness*

℘

PERHAPS the most significant aspect of the Women's Liberation Movement is the premise that woman can perform manual labor equal to that of man at equal pay. The interesting part of this premise is that she comes closer to it than man cares to believe. Obviously, she is not in size the physically strong animal that man is, but pound for pound there would not be a great deal of difference in the work capacity factor of both sexes.

Among the early Indians, women bore the brunt of camp labor. It is not entirely a facetious remark that the Indian woman was expected to walk thirty feet behind her man and carry the pack. It was beneath the dignity of the Indian hunter to perform common camp chores. Often in Indian camps and reservations one sees a woman swinging an ax, though she does this the least well of all her tasks. Tanning hides, a grueling labor, is performed by the Indian women. In the early Southwest where adobe was, and still is, the basic

"Among the early Indians, women bore the brunt of camp labor."

building material for shelter, native women annually applied
the maintenance coat of caliche mud to the outside of dwelling walls with bare hands.

At one time I asked a mother of three children to keep a
pedometer pinned on her from the moment she arose in the
morning until she retired at night. Her day averaged twelve
miles, a distance that her husband could, no doubt, have accomplished in a day's hike; but he in most instances does not,
and I am sure would at the end of the day slump into a chair,
worn to a frazzle.

Europeans are generally of the opinion that American women are pampered. Perhaps most American women *are* pampered. It is one of the luxurious indulgences of men to think of their wives as sexual flowers. Women's hands, apparently, should not look used. A multimillion-dollar hand lotion business sees to that. Calluses? Never!

For many years women were not supposed to be athletic. For them to have muscles suggested physical vulgarity. Subtly beneath all this male-female relationship is the concept of sexual conquest. This may have a primitive origin. Woman pursued by man should run, but not be so athletically endowed that she cannot be caught; or at least, if possessing extraordinary speed, it is expected that she deliberately, though not conspicuously, slow her pace.

Sex will always be confounding. I once knew a farmer who objected strongly to mares pulling a plow. Mares, he said, should be allowed the leisure pasture and do nothing but have their foals. This, while farfetched, is not too removed from most men's solicitude for their women. To help them up over a curb, into a car, carry their packages, and otherwise carry on physical pampering, has been attributed to gallantry. And gallantry I am sure one should practice, though not perhaps by having women assume the common role of physical invalidism. Is not the picture of a woman bouncing with health and vigor springing lightly into the seat of a car, or over a curb, a far more refreshing sight—and if you will, a better sex symbol?

For ten years I conducted wilderness programs in two of America's youth camps—one for boys, the other for girls, involving about six hundred campers and over a hundred counselors. Since it cost more than what the average budget could afford, the youngsters in these camps were largely from the upper-income-bracket families. This affluence might imply that the girls were a money-pampered lot. Some were. Most were not. Part of the program was devoted to canoe trips into the Canadian wilds. Another program involved horseback riding and pack-horse trips. Still another was rifle shooting competition.

My involvement with these two camps in wilderness activity—one program training youngsters, both boys and girls, for Canadian canoe trips and another program training them to pack horses for western mountain trips—revealed some interesting factors where the physical ability of the two sexes was concerned. I must admit that at first I derived some unexpressed amusement in watching young girls from wealthy families wielding manure forks in horse barns. And when I had to allay the aroused fears of overfastidious women counselors and parents as to what girls would do without bathroom facilities in the wilderness, I simply informed them that the little trench shovel was ever handy, and that bushes for privacy were very abundant on the Precambrian shield of Canada. One program director from a finishing school tried to inaugurate side-saddle horseback riding, but she found her horseback riding proselytes with their legs spread over a western saddle, their feet in the stirrups, and no amount of inducement or finishing-school coercion had any effect in changing the western riding style.

On visiting days at the girls' camp, parents and other adults were surprised to see that gallantry had flown when I objected to men visitors helping girl campers and counselors carry canoes to the waterfront for exhibition purposes.

"Why," they remarked reproachfully, "look at that big strong man refusing to help those girls!"

And when a saddle horse got a bit out of hand, spooked by some activity nearby, and an objection by girl counselors arose to any men rushing in to help, all spectators seemed aghast. Getting out of a tough spot was part of the girls' program. After ten years as a director, I haven't seen the girls fail to cope with most situations.

What kind of campers do women make? Women can swing a golf club and wield a paddle, but for some strange reason they have serious trouble in properly swinging an ax. This became such a problem among women counselors that I had to initiate the small Swedish saw for woodcutting on camping and canoe trips. As to the preparation of food over a campfire, if there is something inherent here, girls in organized camps seem to do a much better job than boys with equal experience. It might be said that basically a boy fumbles the camp cook job as badly as a girl swings an ax, though the adult male is generally the "professional" restaurant cook. If you can weave into this strange phenomenon answers to particular innate tendencies in each sex, you have accomplished more than I have done in ten years of watching the relative capabilities of boy and girl campers. Perhaps the answers to these questions will explain the overall reason why the female since time immemorial has inherited the domestic chores, and why the male has had to go afield to perform most other essential functions.

To presume that women cannot adapt to wilderness life is, of course, fallacious. I know a man who sincerely would like to take his wife on his wilderness trips, but he has not done so because, he says, "It's too hard a life for a woman." This can best be summed up in the dialogue I once heard between resort operators and a conservation group in the effort to preserve the Superior National Forest.

Said the resort operator, "Camping is for kids."

"Agreed," replied the conservation representative, "but also for *he*-men and *hearty* women."

Part of the difficulty in analyzing the adaptability of both sexes to wilderness activity is that when men adjust badly, we attribute it to the aversion or incompetence of the particular individual; when women adjust badly, we attribute it to the "inadequacy" of their sex.

The common impression that Indian women make the adjustment to wilderness life because they are Indians is another fallacy, though long empirical adjustment plays a big part here. At least it is a tragic admission of white feminine maladroitness, because Indian women capable of adjustment to the wilderness have shown that they can, with about the same average, grace a drawing room as readily as any Caucasian belle.

On Gunflint Lake, bordering on the Canada–United States

boundary in Minnesota, are two well-known women guides, one an Indian, the other a white woman. In my organized camp program I employed the Indian woman guide to train white camp counselors, not because she was more capable than the white woman guide, but for the valuable ethnic interest she provided. Before the season was over my own white counselors were guiding youth groups into the Canadian wilderness, and doing well at it.

An interesting case of adjustment by an Indian girl should be cited here for emphasis. While I had a cabin on Sea Gull Lake in the Superior National Forest, I was troubled by a large vandalistic black bear. Whenever I returned to the cabin from canoe trips or other absences of any substantial period of time, I was sure to find one of the small buildings clawed into by this bear. As a wildlife conservation measure, I tolerated the damage for some time, hoping that the bear might eventually find a more remote "territorial imperative" on which to carry on his devastation. Finally I concluded that I would have to shoot it.

To get rid of four to five hundred pounds of carrion which I could not utilize, I announced at the trading post a few miles away that I planned to shoot a bear, and inquired if anyone could use it. In the store at the time were a few people, including an elderly Indian woman and a companion Indian girl about eighteen. Both were dressed as though they had been outside on a trip into the conventional world. The girl was in high-heeled shoes and all other attributes of chic attire. Besides, she had that body form which does justice to the clothes of a vibrantly alive young woman. When I addressed my inquiry to those present, I expected some man to approach me and was surprised to find, after a moment of consultation between the Indian girl and elderly Indian woman, that the young Indian girl made the approach.

"You have a bear?" she asked.

"I will have," I said, "but I have to shoot it first. It's raising hell with my place."

"We will take it if you like," she responded.

Three days later I again went to the post and left a message for the Indians to come and get the dead bear. I now had it hanging from a limb, strung up with block and tackle. What I expected was possibly a couple of male Indians to arrive and take away the bear. Instead, that trim young Indian girl I had met in the post pulled up alone in a canoe to my cabin shore. She was dressed in blue jeans, cotton shirt, Indian moccasins and moccasin rubbers, while a red bandanna handkerchief was wrapped around her head, two corner tails of the handkerchief trailing effectively at the back of her neck. The canoe was a Peterborough, in which were several empty fifty-pound-size lard cans and some birchbark pack baskets.

The natural procedure, of course, was to help her get the carcass skinned out, cut up and loaded into the canoe, but she would have no part of my offered help. She made it emphatically clear that it was a woman's job. Whetting her knife now and then, she dropped the skin from that carcass with incredible facility, tied it up and carried it to the canoe. The intestines went into the lard cans to be used, she said, for sled-dog feed, while the meat, packed in the birchbark baskets, would be smoked and used for human food.

Her words were few during the entire procedure, my questions being answered courteously but briefly. I thought it only hospitable to make ready some lunch and beverage for the time when she had completed her job. We sat on a large flat granite formation to eat the lunch. The moment it was over she took the dishes to the lake, washed them, picked up a paddle, and was gone. As I watched her lithe body movements and her canoe paddle flash in the autumn sun down the lake, I could easily understand how so many white men of the North had taken to themselves Indian women.

My wife and I met on an indoor skating rink. It was the kind of rink where one moved at a fast pace on speed skates on the perimeter of a vast oval sheet of ice, a band playing for the rhythm of strokes, while in the center of the ice, others less energetically figure-skated. For my wife and me it was speed skating. I would calculate on occasion how far we

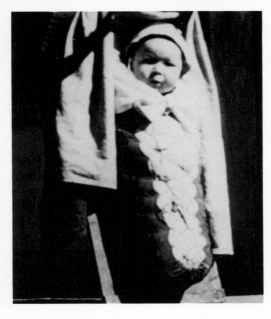

Indian baby in tikinakun.

would have skated in an evening, had the multiple ovals covered been laid out in a single line. The distance totaled between seventeen and twenty miles. I thought about this many times when my wife and I were on snowshoe trails in the Far North. "Do you think you could have done this," I asked her, "if you did not have those skating legs?"

The first trek we made behind a dog sled, and alternately breaking trail for the team, gave the answer. We had covered between ten and twelve miles that first day in soft, hard-going snow. I was glad to get into camp. We had not spoken much for the past five miles. The dogs seemed to be having a hard time even when we had broken trail for them with snowshoes. Once the fire was going in camp I hung a large pail of dog feed on a dingle stick over a separate campfire. And then, in an interval, the answer to the question about good legs came from "the weaker sex." "Why don't you stretch out," said my wife, "while I make something to eat?"

Any question about the adaptability of women to wilderness activity is answered in a day of living with a few Indian families on an island, in a camp, or on the trail. To watch them making camp, smoking meat and fish, making and repairing moccasins, all with a facility so natural—one wonders why the human need has been encumbered with mechanization.

Tiny Indian babies in a wilderness camp seem as well adjusted. They hang in their *tikinakuns* (Indian cradles) on the limbs of trees, swaying with the wind, apparently as contented alone much of their time as they are with their mothers. They are couched within their *tikinakuns* in caribou moss. As to any sympathy extended by white mothers who have their own babies couched in such trade products as Pampers and fluffy soft blankets, they can quiet their concern. Dry caribou moss is one of the most valuable of all desiccants. If you are familiar with silica gel, those particles which come in small pillowlike packages inserted in the containers of fine mechanical instruments to prevent rust by the highly absorbent quality of this substance, you will have a fairly good notion of what the Indian baby is couched in when he is bedded into the highly absorbent caribou moss. When the modern mother disposes of the Pamper, she is doing pretty much what the Indian mother has done down through the ages in disposing of the caribou moss.

I have on occasion watched this "diaper" change, much to the amusement of Indian women. A wood fire is built, and the moss is removed from the *tikinakun* and cast into the fire. Baby, flinching, kicking, and flailing its arms from immersion into the river or lake for a bath, grimaces for a moment from the cold water, but scarcely ever cries. A half dozen babies and mothers at the water's edge, mothers amused by the reaction of the babies to the cool water as they are dunked, creates a kind of merriment that endears these people to one. To see the babies being dried around the fire is another act in the drama. As fire has forever fascinated man, just as instinctively does the baby seem to react to the beauty and warmth of the flames. If babies chuckle in comfort and security in Pampers and flannel blankets with "more time" (for mothers) "to love their babies," so do Indian babies chuckle comfortably and securely in their caribou moss packed *tikinakuns*.

9. *The Alien Wilderness*

A FEW YEARS ago I accompanied a game warden to the banks of the St. Croix River on his invitation to watch him turn loose a racoon that had since birth been illegally kept in a pen. We carried the animal to the river's edge in the wooden crate that had been used to coop it. The entrance closure once removed, the racoon was free to leave, but it did not. It obviously had a feeling of security in staying where it had been all of its life. I thought about the youngster with his "security blanket" in a threatening world, or the canary, caged to sing about nothing in his life that could invoke a song.

The reaction of this racoon to his confinement may be considered parallel to the urbanized human population, who look upon the wilderness as an environment alien to their urbanized, pent-up existence. I have, now and then, been asked, "How did you get interested in the wilderness?" as though it were a radical deviation from the existential "propriety" of man.

Though the game warden soon departed for other duties, I pitched a tent to watch the racoon throughout the remaining part of the day and well into the next—a significant study, I thought, in the rehabilitation of a wild creature. Frightened in the strange, natural environment, it did manage to leave the cage, but came to my tent where I fed it. Human beings had been the only other creatures it had known. The feeding offered an opportunity for me to get rid of the wooden cage. I burned it to compel the animal to seek a natural environment. At the river's edge I gathered some clams and opened several to initiate the racoon to this new diet. Though strange to this domesticated creature, clams are the chief fare for racoons in this river area. The following morning the poor forlorn creature was sleeping in the cold ashes of its lifelong cage. By a little abusive provocation I finally managed to chase it up a tree, but it soon came down to me again. I knew that I had made some progress in orienting it to a natural environment when adeptly it opened, and fed on, the clams which I had gathered. Later it hunted up a few of its own forage. The second day of my observation, the racoon headed up river, and didn't return. I was sure that before long it would find its kindred species.

Some years later I invited a man on a wilderness canoe trip who had never been off New York's Manhattan Island. If there was any difference in the first reaction of both racoon and man to the wilds, it was certainly not in the initiation. Both seemed alien to the wilderness. I shall presume that the racoon soon adapted to the natural environment, and I know that the Manhattan Islander eventually became a wilderness enthusiast.

Thus to most people, in attitude, the wilderness remains a thing apart, today as much as in the early history; surely there is no late attitudinal improvement, with seventy percent of our population well removed from any significant contact with natural environments.

John Muir, whom we might aptly refer to as Mr. Wilderness, fought his way through much opposition as he pursued his passion for "everything . . . wild." Perhaps the greatest obstacle to his natural pursuit was his father, steeped in Calvinistic Christianity, who regarded the wilderness as a sinful waste. There was no plausible reason, the elder Daniel Muir insisted, for an interest in nature beyond the sphere of the ax and the plow. This has not been uncommon. The pioneer, whom we prefer to laud far beyond his commendable stature, was a rare individual indeed if he did not look upon the surrounding wilderness as his natural enemy.

John Muir, only ten when his family left Scotland and settled on a Wisconsin homestead, thus came by his wilderness initiation early. Indians roamed the area at that time, which to the elder Daniel was not of ethnic and cultural interest but only further amplification of his growing composite wilderness antagonism.

To his son, John, all was different. John Muir called it "that glorious Wisconsin wilderness." If ever a generation gap existed, it was between Daniel and his son. To punish John for his profound devotion to natural phenomena, Daniel compelled him to devote all of his time not employed with plow and ax to memorizing the Bible. To Daniel there was no religion in nature. Religion had to be dogmatism, a fetish or nothing.

This was 1849, a time when already Daniel Muir might have had an argument on this score had he taken a cue from Estwick Evans, who in 1818 said: "There is something in the very name of wilderness, which charms the ear, and soothes the spirit of man. There is religion in it." A quotation which, depending on the deletion or inclusion of the last sentence, might readily be adapted to both secular and religious persuasions.

Most writers purport to show that the early regard for wilderness as a sinful waste, a chaotic wasteland, or otherwise as sinister, was due to its inhibitory effect upon the pioneer's survival. Forests were in the way of agriculture, so the trees should be cut or burned. Lumbermen buying a few forties and stealing the timber from a hundred others nearby, accommodated this desire with a devastation that has become an environmental scourge. "Conquer the wilderness" was the phrase that dominated Europeans once they were upon the North American shores. The wilderness as enemy, as villain, as inhibitor to survival, echoed from platform and pulpit.

If history were realistically rewritten, one wonders just what the facts would be. It is true the early majority of the population feared the wilderness. It is also true that the present-day majority, in one degree or another, fear it as much. But what needs to be injected into the realism of history is that avarice and boobery have always dominated the activity of most men where ecology is concerned, and any propaganda slogans that would be saleable to meet the ends of avarice were whooped up wherever expression had a voice. We have the same pattern today. The minority do fight to save the wilderness. The majority seek to destroy the last vestige of it, despite the fact that ecologically they cannot possibly survive without it, though few can be made to understand why this is so.

Whether in science, philosphy, or any other intellectual category, the least seems to be known about the indispensable need of wilderness for preventing man's extinction. Material and monetary values have been and still are the most absorbing educational attractions.

A large share of the fiction pertaining to the wilderness is such gross perversion as to make one wonder whether it has been written through ignorance or the perpetration of deliberate literary fraud to gain more readers. James Oliver Curwood, for example, conjured up such nonsensical scenes as timber wolf packs surrounding the campfires of woodsmen and held at bay only by the constant hurling of flaming fagots toward them, when in reality it is almost impossible to get even a single distant glimpse of a timber wolf over a lifetime in a country well populated with them. Attacks upon human

beings by wolves have been proved through extensive research to be mere fictional fancy.

Perhaps the greatest irony which has been visited upon man
is the basic fact that wherever there is action there inevitably
follows a complement reaction. The harder, for example, one
squeezes a handful of mercury to secure it against loss, the
more readily it squirts out of control between one's fingers.
Or, socially, for a more general and less metaphoric case, the
greater the repressive measures, the sooner revolution. Considering our natural environment on this premise, it did not
occur to me in my early travels in the wilderness that the
inexorable human forces over the world which were determined to exploit the wilderness to its fullest would be set back
on their heels by the very law of nature itself. The so-called
conquest of the wilderness turned out to be not a victory over
opposing forces but a boomerang. If the boomerang does not
threaten human extinction, it has, at least, become a kind of
unexpected environmental mayhem upon man. Perhaps the
most tragic aspect of the war upon the wilderness is that by
our incessant ravages, we haven't as yet acquired even enough
sense to bind up the ecological wounds of a "foe" who proved
to be a friend.

Problems do not, in our resourcefulness, confound us too
often to the point where there seems to be no available answer
or solution. Some sort of hypothetical solution, at least, is
generally had. I have never arrived at an answer as to why
only a small percentage of the human population love the
phenomenon of our natural environment, find it inordinately
friendly and durably satisfying, while the vast majority hate
it, fear it, and run from it. Less than one-half of one percent
of the population enter the wilderness to enjoy, defend, and
protect it. The majority are bent on ravaging it completely.

It is upon this small percentage of affection for the wilderness that we now must depend to save our remaining wild
areas. While we do have some wilderness left, we are facing
the tragic fact that much of it cannot be saved. The ethyl

mercury that has been dumped into rivers, lakes, and oceans, destroying the fish food supply over the world, would take several thousand years to correct itself even if ethyl mercury pollution stopped today. The madness of mercury and other dumping continues for whatever monetary gain can be salvaged from the final catastrophe. What does it matter, we should ask, if in the final analysis we gain vast monetary fortunes and lose human existence?

10. The Micro-Wilderness

ONE OF MY neighbors here on the St. Croix River, less than an hour's drive from Minneapolis and St. Paul, has about an acre plot for his modern residence. Most of it is in lawn and cultivated flower gardens. But a small portion of it, about half of a city-sized lot, is kept wild. It is just as wild, perhaps, where vegetation alone is concerned, as it was hundreds of years ago in its most primal state. In that small wild patch one can watch, from its perimeter, the annual unfolding of seasons, see spring flowers perpetuate their bloom through centuries, note natural decay in the accumulation of humus, observe birdlife seeking sanctuary, and other small wildlife enforcing its territorial imperative—though micro, a wilderness in all its pristine glory.

Will the time come when we will have only such micro-wildernesses? I hope not. I have often discussed my neighbor's micro-wilderness with him. What he points out is that for any area to be classified as a wilderness, man must be prohibited from "developing it," he must not have a hand in it, he must leave it completely alone for maximum enjoyment. Whenever man has interfered by his "developing" process, he has developed the wilderness aspect of it out of existence; in short, destroyed it. The insane notion that wilderness areas should have "multiple use," whenever applied, interrupts or terminates the ecological process—the inter-relationship of every natural element with every form of life in that environment.

Jack Paar once suggested a basic philosophy: "Leave people to hell alone." Grammatically you might quarrel with this statement, and there may be a moot question as to what is meant by leaving people alone, but in essence it has much merit in people interacting happily with people. I would apply this basic concept where natural areas are concerned. If we leave areas "to hell alone," they go round the seasons with a rewarding fruitfulness beneficial to all life on earth. When we interfere we break an ecological chain somewhere that results only in ravage.

On the North Shore of Lake Superior there is an area where you can still see a grove of white pine. It is a consolidated district of wilderness cabins, called Encampment. Highway 61 skirts its perimeter and passes through a part of it. The surprise comes when, as you are speeding along in a car, the pervading coniferous growth of spruce, balsam, and cedar, along with the deciduous growth of birch and moose maple, suddenly gives way to a magnificent forest of towering white pine; and in less than a mile the virgin pine are left behind, the route for hundreds of miles again being spruce, balsam, and deciduous growth.

A large part of the North Shore at one time was an overwhelmingly beautiful spectacle of white and Norway pine, standing conspicuously above other, lesser trees. Had this forest been intelligently cut, it could have gone on forever. By some quirk in the otherwise timber-cutting avarice, a few imaginative people saw fit to preserve this Encampment area to illustrate what ecological sanity can do for our enjoyment.

Every so often the consolidated Encampment area is approached by lumbermen who ask to buy the trees and cut them for lumber. If I gave a dialogue of the verbal exchange that takes place at such times, the editor would for the sake of literary decorum be compelled to delete it, so I leave to the imagination of the reader what might be said by forest-loving people to ravage-minded lumber solicitors. I overheard only one such dialogue at a resort in Itasca County, Minnesota, that had a similar stand of Norway pine towering over the immediate area. The effusive dialogue that took place ended with the following:

The lumberman: "Those trees will mature and eventually die anyway."

The resort operator: "So will you, and the sooner the better for humanity."

I have passed through that area for the past fifty years since that dialogue took place. The micro-forest of Norway pine still stands, apparently new generations of trees reaching for the sky, as a tree here and a tree there matures and dies.

One segment of a private tract in the Rocky Mountains where the owner had a cabin was never explored by him, he said, because he wanted it to remain mysterious and enchanting. Another said, "No man has sufficient mental scope to give a full account of the natural phenomena contained in an acre of wild earth."

There was a time before the advent of the income tax when movie stars made so much money they were at a loss to know how to handle it. Some of them bought ranches and indulged in such fanciful commerce as the breeding of blooded stock, the mere raising of cattle for beef, apparently, being a bit too mundane. One of these stars bought a substantial area in the West for the prime purpose of keeping it wild. Fortunately, it had been left in its original inviolate state, and it promises to remain so by the designation of the recorded will. It is ruggedly fenced against grazing encroachment of neighboring cattle herds, and patrolled to prevent the ravage of its wildlife by hunters.

What stands out beyond all other highly significant factors is that it disproves the validity of the phrase *multiple use*.

The great Norways of yesteryear.

Adjoining regions treated as multiple-use areas stand in semi-sterile, grim contrast to what they might have been, had they been left to the natural processes. The area has become a kind of private sanctuary where ecologists, biologists, and others can see and study an area not exploited for monetary profit.

Since the area is quite extensive—probably the outer limits of what could be considered a micro-wilderness—it is looked upon covetously by ranchers and other profit-minded entrepreneurs.

The whole defense of such micro-wilderness areas is not accomplished by multistrand barbed-wire fences. Verbal and legal attacks also have to be met. Every conceivable effort has been made to get such areas released for hunters and for grazing. The argument that hunting is needed in the area to keep a balance in wildlife populations becomes incessant and is, of course, false ecology. Hunters seek to kill healthy animals, and thus only diminish the vigor of those remaining. Left alone, predators kill off the weak and the old, to keep up the vigor of those remaining. The argument by ranchers that with an increase in human population, the world needs food and the area should be grazed by cattle instead of wild creatures, gets short shrift in the logical answer from the owners. "Cut back the population by every conceivable means of liberalized birth control, abortion, and family planning before you destroy the whole of life everywhere."

As national forests, national parks, state camp grounds are surrounded by the encroaching population, they become only micro-wildernesses. Their wilderness aspect, especially the smaller areas, is difficult to preserve against the onslaught of blacktop highways, demands for hunting, and the reckless slashing instead of intelligent cutting of timber. Yet, there is hopefully a growing consciousness, though still feeble, that we cannot survive without these wilderness areas.

On the tar-and-gravel roof of a metropolitan apartment building, I saw a cement mortar mixing box in which a tenant had planted some evergreen-tree seedlings and a few square feet of moss. The seedlings were dead, the moss struggled for life, though watered daily. I talked to the tenant about his micro-wilderness.

"It's no use," he said; "death is in the air here in the city."

There is much current rhetoric about the indispensable need of wilderness for man to survive. But here we are talking primarily about physical survival. The thought occurs to me that if we are so in need of a daily glimpse of a few tree seedlings in a mortar box, an occasional bouquet of flowers on a birthday, or a geranium on the window sill, physical survival may not be the only important factor in sustaining life. There may be an inscrutable need for at least the micro-wilderness, to sustain the better part of our mental health as well as our physical well-being.

11. Legend of a Woodsman

THE TWENTIETH century stands unique in history for its radical transition. There were—and will, of course, be—transitions of sorts in any century. But those which took place before the twentieth were only of steady evolution, and despite promising industrial change, those beyond the twentieth will likely also be in steady evolution. No century can be expected to have the radical change of the twentieth. The nineteenth century and those earlier were largely of the manual order, whereas the twentieth suddenly went from the manual to the mechanized. The back country was wilderness before the turn of the twentieth, much of it unexplored where no white man had ever trodden. To the young it will seem strange that early in the twentieth there were no radios or television sets, that the automobile was a clumsy experiment over mud-mired roads. The wilderness had not heard the roar of the chain saw, the outboard motor, the snowmobile, and rarely the plane. Gas and kerosene lamps illuminated the streets, the home, and cabin. Most railways cutting through a vast wilderness were being built by horse-drawn dirt scrapers, hand shovels, and black powder instead of dynamite to blast out the rock cuts.

"To have been or not to have been" a part of the early life takes on a wholly different cast than "to be or not to be" a part of current life. And "that is the question" we might consider here.

To best make the distinction, presume for a moment what your life would be today, were people suddenly to awake one morning faced with this reversal: no cars or blacktop highways; no electricity in the home; no planes, outboard motors, or snowmobiles; no refrigeration except the icebox—in short, cut back mechanization drastically and substitute manual effort for most mechanical work. That was the situation at the turn of the century.

Just to speculate on such modification in the local scene has to astound even those of us who experienced the transition. The cities of Minneapolis and St. Paul early in the century seemed to me at the time stupendous metropolises. But the suburbs of these cities—where now are strung great four-lane highways and massive shopping districts—were the weekend tramping grounds for outdoor enthusiasts, where a tent could be set up along a then freshwater stream, the predominant sounds being the babbling brook and the wind in the trees.

The Mississippi River and Minnehaha Creek near Minneapolis and St. Paul had great possibilities as wild areas, as I have described in my book *Challenge of the Wilderness*. But perhaps the "ultima Thule" of local exploration nearest the cities was the St. Croix River, the dividing line between Minnesota and Wisconsin. Nature had the canoeist in mind when it created the St. Croix. The current is not too fast but that a canoe can be paddled upstream. While many small trout streams flow into the St. Croix, the great charm of its banks comes from thousands of crystal-clear springs that empty into the river, where small-mouth bass, especially abundant in those earlier days, lay waiting for food and as readily became the victim of an artificial yellow-sal fly cast by a fisherman.

Lumbermen who cut the white pine missed many young trees which grew up to blend with a magnificent hard- and softwood forest of basswood, ironwood, ash, sugar maple,

"Nature had the canoeist in mind when it created the St. Croix."

hickory, and other tree species. One could pitch a tent on any of innumerable rock and soil shelves, under stands of white pine, alongside a spring-fed stream. The ironwood cooking fires could be so small by virtue of the intense heat generated by this hard wood that a slim pole from a small, dead tree was ample fuel for days of cooking. Ironwood was the choice wood for making carpenter chisel handles, and other uses requiring a bone-hard, tough wood. For this reason, one had qualms about burning it, though it grew in abundance.

On Sunday there was the occasional canoe party on the river, but for the balance of the week, one scarcely saw even the wilderness devotee. It was on an early trek up the St. Croix on foot with a pack that I met John, a woodsman of rare character. He was sixty seven years of age when first I knew him. His actions, his outlook, and his appearance belied his age. John had never been to a public school. Somehow his rearing in a remote Wisconsin wilderness region didn't lend this opportunity. But his mother had filled the educational gap. She had taught him what he needed to know for a practical living at least—the three Rs. And she had laid the foundation for his vocation when she taught the boys in the family to cut one another's hair. In time John became so good at it, he got the occasional head of hair to trim for a fee outside the family.

But John was not a barber at heart. He, like John Muir, loved the wilds too much. When I met John he was camped on a wide, forested rock shelf of the St. Croix River where Silver Creek empties into it, about six miles above the earliest settlement in Minnesota, Marine on St. Croix. I had already hiked sixteen miles along the river with a pack as I came onto his camp, and welcomed a stop. John was sitting on a stump near a cooking fire, frying brook trout. Intent upon what he was doing and scarcely looking up, he said, "You're just in time."

My formal apologies for intruding on his camp were not met with the usual assurances of welcome that one might expect. Without stirring, he growled, "If you didn't smell trout frying two miles down river in this wind you need a nose operation. You'll find a tin plate and cup inside the tent."

For a moment I was at a loss to know whether I was merely being tolerated as a nuisance guest, or whether this—which I learned later to be true—was his brand of humor. We sat on packing boxes and ate from a table made of driftwood lumber that had been salvaged from the river during the spring flood. I had accidentally come upon the camp of one of the great woodsmen of that time, John Campbell.

Young, strong, youthfully impressionable, signed and sealed in my own mind to the wilderness, I felt an exaltation in this woodsman's presence. Eating trout and bannock, drinking tea, and absorbing the grandeur of the autumnal forest brilliant in fall colors, while Silver Creek audibly danced over its gravel- and boulder-strewn bottom nearby, I felt a sense of profound well-being. The St. Croix River's voluminous flow was salmon-colored in the evening sun. A breeze quaked the leaves overhead at times, as gusts skipped across the smooth-flowing waters of the river, leaving a wake of ripples behind, and finally dissipating in the opposite forested shore.

John's camp was semipermanent, not the light, mobile type. It consisted of two rather large, heavy canvas wall tents. Inside one was another table and some benches made from driftwood lumber. Brilliant-colored Hudson's Bay blankets covered two folding-type camp cots. A rifle with a sling and a fishing rod hung from the tent's center pole. A wood-burning camp cook stove, with its pipe going up through a tent thimble, suggested comfort on chilly fall mornings. A small tree actually rooted in the ground, its branches short-cropped, "grew" in one corner of the tent. On this natural "clothes tree" hung various items of clothing, field glasses, and other paraphernalia. A thick layer of white cedar boughs covered the floor, giving off a spicy, coniferous fragrance and providing a soft, carpetlike cushioning underfoot. In the second tent was a tool chest propped off the ground, a work bench, canoe paddles, snowshoes, and various other equipment pertinent to wilderness life.

Only fifty miles from Minneapolis and St. Paul, John's campsite would scarcely be considered remote or wild today, though it was quite isolated early in the century. To reach the spot demanded ruggedness to carry a pack overland, or doing what John did in transporting his heavier camp gear—find a river town that could be reached by rail and float down to the campsite in a canoe. This, of course, is what John did on getting his camp set up in the spring; but his ingenuity was extended beyond such common application when he chose to go "outside" for any reason, and he had definite basic reasons for going outside, as will be seen.

John knew on which side his bread was buttered. He knew the practicability of playing his hand on the side of affluence. My own situation was closer to austerity than affluence at that time, yet John accepted me as he accepted the stream that flowed by his camp, or the wind in the trees. A rapport quickly developed between us. He lived much as I did, not on a round-the-year income from employment, but on employment enough for a grubstake, and the bare qualitative equipment needed to sustain wilderness life. We could, as time went on, depend on each other for companionship, though we did not exactly form a wilderness partnership. My independent spirit would not allow that, nor would his. As the seasons moved in and out, we were much together on the St. Croix and in the Far North. It might be said that our trails divided periodically when he went on his way to provide his strange kind of subsistence—unique by any standards of either the wilderness or metropolitan life.

For example, during the berry season he would gather enough wild fruit to make both jams and wine. But these were not ordinary items. He told me about the delicate preserves and the fine wines his mother made, in which the whole family in season was annually engaged, both in the picking of the berries and the making of the end product. So far, this may appear to have no extraordinary aspect. The incredible part of John's wilderness preserves- and wine-making lay in his marketing procedure. Underlying the marketing was his unique people-engaging appeal. One might think that for effect in selling his products he would be dressed in buckskins and simulate a Daniel Boone in costume by virtue of his wilderness life. And I hasten to add that a good deal of the time when he was in the wilds, he did have such dress. While such dress, naturally, would arouse curiosity in the city, John reasoned—and wisely—that it would not be compatible with marketing delicate preserves and fine wines, if he were to impart the effect of scrupulous sanitation.

When John went into the city to make the contacts to sell his products, he dressed in clothes that at that time would more likely have been worn by an affluent Scotchman on a golf course. His knickers, deeply-ribbed wool stockings, moccasin-type oxfords of rich chestnut color, complement coat and cap, set him off from both the conventional crowd and the man of the wilderness, not gaudily but with an eye-catching distinction. How he managed without membership to gain access to the lounging rooms of the finest clubs, besides also spending time and becoming an accepted figure in the best hotel lobbies, I never fully learned. But acceptance he managed, and contacts he made, among the affluent society. If clothes and circumstance initiated the contacts, then his fantastic tales of the wilderness held the novelty-seeking rich spellbound. Let it be said that he made no pretense at affluence himself. "I am not regarded as one of them," he said. "To them I am an interesting character."

In conversations with his hosts he subtly managed to inject the legend of the extraordinary skill his family had as a tradition in making delicate wild preserves and fine wild wines. And in the stories he told his hosts, there was no hint that the stock of these products would be distributed as gifts. Far from it. His small jars of wild preserves, which he carried in what might be described as a "pantry packsack," sold for fabulous prices. His wild wines in ordinary wine-size bottles he priced so high, it left me at the time dumbfounded. Who would pay such prices? The esoteric-seeking rich, of course, who wanted to impress their friends.

The extraordinary part of these wilderness fruit preserves and wines was that at these high prices he never had enough to fill the demand. Bound up in the whole of John's character and his contact with affluent society was not only the wilderness rarity of his wines and jams but the elements of novelty and atmosphere he brought with him—something that kept ennui and boredom at bay, where money too often bought everything but happiness. On various occasions John would mail jars of preserves to someone requesting them, and enclose a memo of the price and postage. Later, instead of the asked price, he often got back a check for several times the amount. One day he picked up a package that had arrived by express. It proved to be the gift of a fine imported English rifle and a Hardy rod from England, sent by a wealthy American family touring Europe.

John's repertoire of stories and his seemingly natural sense of humor were never overplayed, so that when a bit of levity was needed the effect was always good. John needed a canoe. Mine, a birchbark made for me by an Indian at Mille Lacs, was left with him at times for his convenience; but when I needed it, John was for the time deprived. On one of my visits I noticed that he had a commercially made, natural-cedar-finish canoe which he was varnishing. He explained that it had come floating down the river on the spring flowage. Where from, with a hundred miles of river and as many tributaries, we never learned. "Aren't you lucky," I said, since it was really a fine craft.

"Not so lucky," retorted John, "there weren't any paddles in it."

When the moose season was still open in Minnesota in those days, John guided affluent hunters. Each fall I helped him decamp and paddle the load to Osceola, Wisconsin, where it was put on a train for the North Country.

One of these hunting clients was a prominent doctor. The

ten-day package arrangement John made with those he guided was paid in advance, and applied in full no matter how soon they got their moose and departed. The doctor shot one the first day and made overtures toward leaving for the city. Obviously, he personally wanted to show off the moose, rather than send it down to the city. The doctor came up with the excuse that he had some patients who really needed his care. Financially, there was no loss to John with his ten-day guiding package, but to be equitable and friendly, John tried to induce the doctor to stay.

In his usual brusque manner, John said, "Why the hell don't you stay up here, Doc, for the rest of the ten days and give your patients a chance to get well?"

John was never in need of a doctor himself. At a very advanced age he had the nimble step of a young man. On one occasion among some young people he engaged in an informal running-broad-jump contest and won it. I wondered what method the Grim Reaper could possibly apply to John's withdrawal from life. One day it came. I had to take John out of the wilderness to the hospital. He had become desperately ill. The glands in his throat and under his arms were swelled. No professional diagnosis was needed. Malignance was upon him. I was invited to take a seat in one of the Cadillacs that formed the funeral procession. The rich had laid John to rest.

12. *Wilderness Sanctuary*

❦

THERE IS less likelihood that identity can be lost in the wilderness as readily today as it was early in the century. Various means of communication are too far-reaching today. Numerous kinds of patrol—Wildlife Departments, Royal Canadian Mounted Police (RCMP), Departments of Lands and Forests—these and others now have comparatively easy air access to just about every region of the continent. Remoteness once had its value in providing sanctuary. The long canoe- or dog-sled trek by members of the various government wilderness departments was rare. True, patrols were made, even into the upper Arctic, but these were largely "territorial imperative" patrols to guarantee Canada's jurisdiction over those somewhat disputed regions by long occupational rights. And when these patrols were made they were cursory, thousands of square miles lying unobserved—in fact, largely with vague geographical boundaries. Only with the advent of air travel did the boundaries of these lands finally get delineated.

Thus, the vast region, reaching well into the northern and western United States and over most of Canada, became an unmolested sanctuary for many "lost persons." Who these people were and their reasons for wanting wilderness asylum would involve the unraveling of a thousand and one ever-remaining mysteries and social problems.

We continue to find the question moot whether there is to be a greater latitude of permissiveness in individual conduct than the criminal statutes actually allow, or whether all shall obey the law to the letter. The list of lost persons who are major or minor violators of the criminal code, who will never be sought, must indeed be long. While not all violations are outlawed by the time element, many are. Those violations which have interested me as having a strange sociological aspect are where the violator has sought escape from the law by becoming a *wilderness recluse*. I suppose that an in-depth study of profound social significance could also be made for the large number of persons who vanish in the crowd of great urban populations, but they seem to lack the fascination surrounding the wilderness recluse.

A point of significance in the search and prosecution of any violator, whether minor or major, is that in many instances of violation where the individual had been sought and no longer seemed to be in evidence as a further violator, the case is disposed of by the metaphor "Let sleeping dogs lie." In the rather limited, basic themes which go to make up the long list of TV and scenario Western dramas, the theme of the man who had committed an early crime but had since become distinguished and benevolent enough to give a languishing town new life, even though his early crime is known, scarcely ever fails to intrigue an audience and gain its sympathy—a point in the general rehabilitation process of criminals that seems compassionately commendable.

The word *hermit* is largely a misnomer. All men need and want some kind of companionship, but sometimes they have to sacrifice it for one reason or another. In my early solitary travels through the wilderness areas by canoe and dog sled, I came upon strange cases of isolation, and while my presence was avoided on several of these occasions, it was not, apparently, because the avoider did not want company. He most likely, I concluded, feared being identified. It isn't odd, of course, that persons who live isolated wilderness lives should intrigue us. The gregarious nature of man is most often too strong in all of us to allow complete estrangement from our fellow men. Thus, when one finds an individual living alone in a remote wilderness cabin, curiosity regarding his chosen isolation can be very tantalizing.

There is nothing unusual about finding rude log cabins in remote wilderness areas. Most frequently they are trapping cabins, or they have been roughly thrown up as base camps for prospectors. Bark is still on the logs under which ant borers are busy reducing the structure to sawdust. It is also not unusual to find that a bear has made entrance to these cabins by tearing away a part of the roof. But when one comes upon a structurally fine log cabin more than a hundred miles from the railroad, logs peeled, oakum used for chinking, the interior furnished with well-crafted, wilderness-made furniture, shelves of books, chests of clothes, and other valuable items, the first thought is: a recreational cabin belonging to an affluent city dweller who manages periodical stays each year in his wilderness retreat.

It was such a structure that I unexpectedly came onto alone by canoe about mid-afternoon, after a half dozen portages and some rather long paddling since my previous night's camp. The first impulse, naturally, was to learn if it was occupied. I called out from my seat in the canoe, but no answer came. Beaching the canoe, I walked toward the door, whereupon it became apparent at once by the growth in the yard that no feet had been over the lake-to-cabin trail in a long time. Considering that the door might be latched from the inside, I tried it. It swung open easily, but with a slight creaking labor in the hinges that further suggested a lack of occupancy; how long was only a guess.

Two gable ventilating louvers, one at each end of the cabin, had kept the interior dry and fresh. Weary from long travel, I decided to spend the night there rather than pitch another camp. The latchstring usually hung out in remote wilderness cabins for a weary traveler. In the case of the various cabins I have owned in the wilderness, it was not unusual to come back to any of them after an absence and find welcome smoke rising from the chimney.

The nameless lake (many lakes then were nameless) on which the cabin was situated spread like the fingers on one's hand into long bays that continued the waterways into several small rivers. It was obvious why the owner chose to build on this intricate and wide-spreading body of water. Here he had unlimited potentials for a wilderness interest.

An inverted Peterborough cedar canoe, equipped with portaging yoke and paddles, spanned the overhead beams of the cabin. From evidence that I could find in and around the cabin, I tried to determine the probable occupation or interest of the cabin owner. What I wanted to know was likely contained in a locked, handmade chest, the privacy of which, of course, I had to respect.

On the table was a friction-top can containing sugar, and a place setting of plate and cup. In the bottom of the cup was dried coffee; the plate was unwashed. From this I concluded that only one person had occupied the cabin, that while he had eaten what was on his plate, apparently, a whole cup of coffee which had been poured had dried down to leave the existing dry, brown incrustation. If I was to judge from the careful storage of the canoe—unless, of course, there had been more than one, which was unlikely—the occupant had not drowned. Could it be that he had died in the woods? Why had he left the whole cup of coffee dehydrating in the cup, and why had he not washed the dishes? The general order of the cabin seemed too neat to believe that he had left unwashed dishes for a year or more—estimating the lapsed time by the growth around the cabin. The coffee pot also had a brown incrustation in the bottom. Normally, one would not make a pot of coffee, fill a cup, and leave it. When I found stale, dry provisions stored away in metal containers, I finally concluded that the original occupant had been urgently called away and could not return.

It seemed clear that while the cabin was of the finished type, with peeled logs, it probably sat on land belonging to the government; in short, a squatted-on site—which, of course, deep in the wilderness was common procedure in those early days. Had the cabin been permanently abandoned? Presuming that the owner had died, would the heirs be of such character that they would recreationally occupy a cabin almost a hundred miles from the railhead? If not, I speculated, why had they failed to take possession of the personal belongings; and if there had been no relatives, why had not the Provincial authorities taken possession?

These thoughts kept flitting through my mind until I encountered some Indians in two birchbark canoes making a portage to one of the river levels below a falls on a northwest arm of the lake. They had passed the cabin, and disturbance of the vegetation in front of it told them that someone had taken up occupancy. They believed that the owner had returned, but customary Indian modesty, the language barrier, or independence, if you will, kept them from stopping. They lived an additional hundred and fifty miles to the north, and knew by hearsay a few things about the original occupant.

With my meager knowledge of Cree, and their as meager knowledge of English, I managed, nevertheless, to gather the essential fact. The cabin owner was in prison. I was not to know the details until ten days later when I reached the railhead by canoe. There had been a fight. The cabin owner's opponent had been quite seriously injured. A number of the people in the small wilderness settlement were incensed over the jailing of the cabin owner, because they were convinced that he had been defrauded by his opponent and in seeking adjustment of his claim, was provoked into an assault.

Since this was a small railroad settlement of peace-loving,

plain-living people, nobody felt that anything could be done toward having the sentence either reduced or terminated by digging up evidence to show extenuating circumstances. Today, perhaps, under similar circumstances, with vastly increased communications, something would have been learned about the defrauding plaintiff in the trial. The question that dominated the trial was: Had the cabin owner defended himself against an assault by the plaintiff; or as the plaintiff claimed, had a premeditated assault been made upon him? The plaintiff's claim proved later to be false, but his perjured testimony won out at the trial.

Over a year had passed since the cabin owner was sentenced. His sled dogs had been turned over to a close friend in the settlement. Much can be learned about a man from his sled dogs. They seemed to have been raised by gentle hands.

It is not the province of the police to get people out of jail

when they have been legally tried and sentenced. But the authorities, nevertheless, cooperated in a most friendly way when I sought to learn something about the history of the man who apparently had defrauded the cabin owner. When finally I discovered, in tracing his origin, that he actually was wanted in two separate districts for similar frauds, but had never been apprehended or tried, I still didn't think there was too much to go on. Eventually, I found that one of the cases he had been involved in was an assault case similar to that with the cabin owner; and I felt that an effort might now be made to terminate the cabin owner's sentence, or get it reduced.

"Much can be learned about a man from his sled dogs." (A team similar to the trapper's owned by Dr. John E. Frankson—photo by the author.)

Within two weeks enough affidavits and depositions had been collected to make a favorable case.

I had sufficiently ingratiated myself with the people in the settlement, and especially with the cabin owner's friends who cooperated with me in the investigation, to feel comfortable about using the cabin. But litigation is slow and cumbersome. Twice over the ensuing weeks I returned to the settlement by canoe, and on each occasion found only disappointment.

Winter was coming on. The ice along the shore was forming and breaking up with each succeeding wind. Since the cabin owner's sled dogs were being kept in a chicken-wire enclosure and would probably not get ample exercise, they were turned over to me along with a sled. I fed the dogs for almost a week, to get them adjusted to me, before I considered it safe to allow them to run along the shore for the trip back to the cabin. The lead dog, a female, I kept with me in the canoe to increase the chances of having all of the dogs follow. There were times when I had to ferry all of the dogs across long inlets, but as I fed them at various points over the route, they became so attached to the canoe, they swam across quite a few of these inlets and all of the streams. What gave me a great deal of encouragement and confidence as well as amusement was that they seemed to know the route. I had no doubt about their having been over this same route many times before.

Within about twelve miles of the cabin at a wide bay, I lost complete sight of the dogs, though I still had the lead dog in the canoe. Had they suddenly decided to go back to the settlement where they had been for over a year? For the first time I became deeply concerned; nevertheless, I continued on to the cabin. There was, after all, little need for my concern. Several miles from the cabin, out on a rocky point, there they were, looking for me. As the retracing of their tracks indicated, I judged that they might already have been at the cabin. I breathed a sigh of relief, went ashore to give them some tidbits and a friendly rub. Once my canoe was headed toward the cabin they were gone again, and just as I expected, were at the cabin in great anxiety, waiting for me at the water's edge.

As an adjustment period here for the dogs, I let them run loose for the day. The owner had provided a rather roomy chicken-wire-fenced enclosure for them to run in, similar to the one in which they had been kept in the settlement. I considered that they would satisfy themselves that their owner was not about and would make the best of their new keeper.

I now settled down for that no-travel period between open water and freeze-up. The North Country had already gone through the autumn coloring stage, but a vestige of color still remained. The air was crisp and invigorating. There was more than myself to feed, and despite the fact that thin ice formed quite far out and continued to break up with every heavy wind, I kept a net out nightly for a fish supply. Having ranged over much of the water area, I also had a good idea where I would look for a moose, once the weather was cold enough to freeze the meat. Moose seemed to be quite plentiful. During the rutting season there was little trouble calling moose to the waterfront with the use of a birchbark horn, though I was in no position to put up moose meat that early in the season. Then, too, there was the uncertainty of my continued residence in the cabin. What a spectacle to see these magnificent creatures appear on the shore when called!

My last visit at the settlement convinced most of us there that our efforts to free the cabin owner, or at least get his sentence modified, had all been in vain. In fact, we were of the opinion that we were simply being ignored. Each mail packet would carry hope until the mail was sorted and read. Quite certain of failure, I planned to spend the winter in the cabin. I even found a supply of spar varnish which the owner had apparently planned to put on the logs but never got to it. On a sunny day when the temperature took a sudden rise, I put the varnish on with a rag when I couldn't find a brush. I repaired a roof on one of the storage buildings which had been stoved in by a large blown-down white spruce. I put fresh, dry marsh grass in the doghouses and made some repairs of the dog harness. In the meat cache the well-frozen meat of a young moose was stored, though to make certain of preserving it, I covered the cache every day with blankets and boughs to maintain the night freeze through the following day, should there be a thaw.

That final morning came when the lake ice held. The howling wind drove flakes horizontally across it in a white fury. The dogs snuggled in their individual houses, almost lost from sight under the drifting snow. Yet, whenever I left the cabin they broke open the enclosing drifts at the entrance to see what I was up to. Once again back in the cabin, I could see them shaking themselves free of snow and returning to the comfort of their dry marsh-grass beds.

About a foot of snow had accumulated on the level, drifting here and there to several times this height. Prospecting holes had to be cut in the ice for the best winter fishing, along with a water-supply hole, all covered with boughs to prevent their freezing up.

The dogs, once in harness, were as anxious to get going on all-day trips as I was to see those regions which earlier had been less accessible by canoe.

As usual, after the snowfall the temperature dropped rapidly. For almost a week it remained well below zero. Though the wood fire kept the cabin warm, the door hardware inside stayed white with frost. Whenever the temperature rose appreciably above zero, the frost would melt off. Variations of this frostiness became almost as indicative of the outside temperature as the thermometer.

Where the dogs on first arriving at the cabin seemed to be seeking their owner (though this is mere conjecture based on their conduct), they were now apparently becoming resigned to me. A large pail of dog feed had to be cooked each day. In such considerate feeding and care they build a sense of security. One has to be careful not to overdo the petting of sled dogs while they are in harness. On the other hand, a certain amount in the intervals draws them close, keeps them friendly and responsive to one's needs.

For Christmas, on earlier invitation, I had planned to make a trip to the settlement. Preparations had been started a week in advance so as to have proper food on the trail for "mug-ups" and the several overnight camps. I was frying doughnuts for these "mug-ups" when suddenly the dogs in concert began to create a great disturbance. I suspected that possibly a wolverine or other creature had come into the area. But the dogs' focus was not on anything immediate. Far down the lake I dimly made out two dog teams, and assumed that they were an Indian party moving on to their trapping grounds farther to the north. Since the temperature was down, I returned to the cabin and resumed the doughnut frying, glancing out occasionally to see if the sleds were getting nearer. Water was always kept hot on the stove for tea. When the sleds appeared to be heading toward the cabin, I placed a large, cold, already prepared moose roast in the oven to heat for whatever contingency might arise. Hungry, trail-weary men likely would have to be fed. The usual big pail of dog feed also kept on the back of the stove would now, no doubt, have to be diverted to feed strange, trail-worn dogs as well.

In the pandemonium that ensued as the two dog teams and a party of four men drew near the cabin, only the most fragmentary communication between the men and me was possible, but I managed to glean just enough information to get the cardinal news, which was shouted in my ear.

The cabin owner had been freed! He was one of the four men who had arrived.

What the cabin owner's reaction would be to my occupancy of his cabin, I had no idea. I considered some kind of apology for trespassing and was about to suggest this on a humorous note when, moist-eyed and without a word, he warmly embraced me. No words were necessary.

I thought it a good time to issue some hospitable orders: "Let's get the dogs fed, and then come inside for some chow."

I did not observe firsthand what happened when the cabin owner went to visit his dogs. It seemed to be just one more of those situations where a man needs to be alone.

Five men and seventeen dogs spent Christmas at that cabin. Gifts had been brought and exchanged. If Christmas tends to cheer the spirit of men, it was not conventionally necessary in that group. Another bond—man's rational and compassionate interest in man—had welded spirits. I planned to return to the settlement with the Christmas party, but the cabin owner pleaded with me to remain at least until spring. My canoe was there and my yet unsatisfied interest in the area, along with the personality of the cabin owner, decided it. The winter went fast with a rewarding association and experience for me. A day came when great flocks of geese were in flight to the salt flats of James Bay. As I headed south alone in my canoe toward the settlement and began rounding the first obscuring point, I saw the cabin owner wave, then turn on the rocky shore and head for his cabin.

13. No Tale Will Tell

❧

CLOUD WAS a woods Indian. He looked it. His entire grand ancestry testified to it. His every action would have belied any other possible concept. He went through the woods in a movement more accurately described as threading than hiking. I managed to stay with him only by a forced extension of effort. In the saddle as a cowhand on the western range, I should have gained a clue to the secret of his mobility. A rider moves with the rhythm of his mount. In the forest on foot, one moves with the rhythm that contour and obstructions dictate. It is not a deliberate hurdle over each individual obstacle. It is more like the over-and-around, slithering, graceful movement of a snake.

At first I thought, though incorrectly, that Cloud was trying to outdo me. His pace seemed faster than necessary. Behind a dog sled his pace was that of the dogs, not running, not walking—a killing intermediate pace that seemed unnatural to the step of man, at least to mine.

You get some idea of such out-of-white-man-phase of movement when you try to walk the ties of a railroad. The spacing is never right to the step. Some diabolical engineer, I insist, set the mathematical spacing of ties. The secret, I finally learned, of walking a track is to ignore the spacing and let the steps fall where they may, on or off the ties. And the secret of getting over wilderness terrain is likewise to forget your long-developed, even, sidewalk pace and, as it were, roll with the punches, to every length, different height, and different quality of step.

This was part of the adjustment I had to make to Cloud as a wilderness traveling companion.

The first meeting with him was under rather strange circumstances. He was in a North Country settlement trading post, trying to spend the monetary equivalent of a few furs for a pair of coveralls, some moccasin-rubbers, ammunition, and other such needed items. The calculations somehow didn't come out right, at least not in Cloud's favor. He needed a little credit or outside subsidy. The coveralls he wore were so ragged, I could see the muscles of his well-proportioned, strong body rippling through several torn places.

Cloud dickered with the post manager in Cree. When I nodded to the manager and indicated with a few words that I would make up the difference in Cloud's needs, I made the mistake of assuming that Cloud did not understand or speak English. While his was not the King's English, it was, nevertheless, communicable to me.

I wasn't sure that Cloud was accepting this token of help amicably. He turned on me so impulsively I expected offense, and said, "I work for you."

It was a plain case of neither he nor I having any particular work to do or place to go. Cloud had been living off the country. He had a 22-caliber, single-shot, small-game rifle, its once blue finish worn down to raw steel. In a moosehide musette type of bag hung over his shoulder, he carried simple fishing tackle and ammunition. Near the door of the post lay his rabbit-skin blanket rolled in a light canvas tarp. Outside of a knife hung at his belt in a moosehide sheath, ingeniously lined with wood, these items in evidence were his entire worldly possessions—a simplification of life which in the wilderness proves to be more one of affluence than austerity.

Since I didn't need a guide or anyone to work for me, what I saw in Cloud was the possibility of an interesting association, better insight into Indian life; in short, a trail companion. We discussed the arrangement over a pot of tea and some lunch at the water's edge, no more than a hundred feet from the post. On a sandy beach a mile down the lake we stopped and had a plunge and bath. Cloud donned his new coveralls and burned his old ones. Stripped, a bronze figure, he looked more power- ful and athletic than I had at first thought. He swam like a seal.

The new coveralls needed a lot of timeworn assimilation to his body. I told Cloud that he looked too dressed-up.

"I think you should go in swimming," I said, "with your clothes on."

Right then I discovered that Cloud had a great sense of humor, and daring. He took off his moccasins and moccasin- rubbers, hiked to the top of a precipitous rock formation over the water, and dived in with his coveralls on. He was an hour drying out before a fire.

Cloud was determined to earn the "subsidy." Besides, I think he enjoyed flexing his magnificent muscles. It isn't un- common to make a second trip over portages. With Cloud as a companion you had to ask yourself, "Is this second trip neces- sary?" Whatever I failed to take over a portage, he shouldered along with the canoe. While there was little need for expedi- ency or hurry, I found that the mobility factor of getting over a portage trail in one fell swoop added an element of luxury to travel, especially those days when for some reason you wanted to reach a place of particular interest, or get into a more desirable area.

The additional provisions acquired at the post on meeting

Cloud pointed up for me a new food budget approach. While he made no issue of it, the provisions I had purchased at the post, apparently, were largely needless luxuries to him. These were years early in the century when wildlife seemed unlimited, and to live off the country for a woods Indian was as unquestioned as breathing the forest air. Our several packsacks of food for weeks of wilderness travel did not seem to me exorbitant, at the rate of two pounds per day per man. Yet it was, because Cloud made it quite clear to me before long that our diet should be mainly meat and fish. Consequently, after a week of travel we made a cache, and after the second week still another.

Toward the end of the third week we were several hundred miles from our starting point on the Canadian National Railroad. The chance of meeting anyone other than Indians this far from the railroad seemed unlikely. As we skirted the edge of a small lake, Cloud stopped paddling, sniffed the air, and said, "Pustao" (smoke).

The possibility of a forest fire seemed remote after a week of much rain. I was pondering this point when Cloud remarked, "Mekewap" (camp), assuming the pose of one listening for a faintly audible distant sound.

That the Indian innately has senses finer than those of any other race isn't likely; but when he is raised in a strictly wilderness environment, he inevitably trains his senses to function at a finer degree than the urban citizen whose hearing, sight, and smell suffer deterioration from incessant noise and smog. Perhaps the most extraordinary faculty which the Indian in the wilderness develops is his ability to spot some object by contrast. His observations go beyond this. To the untrained eye a distant movement on some shore could be an animal, or no more than the waving of a low branch in the wind—even the shadow of a rock formation shifting from the sun's apparent movement. The distinction is generally made quite readily by the Indian. Whenever something seen was questioned, Cloud came up with the answer, "Mooswu" (moose) or "Kistapisk" (rock), long before I could make that distinction.

The mystery of the smoke was soon made clear. In a cove of the lake we were on, almost hidden, was a log cabin. We might have missed seeing the cabin had it not been for an overturned canoe on the shore, partly obscured by brush, and a very faint wisp of smoke rising from the cabin chimney, dispersing in our direction. We pulled onto the shore. Our voices, being now in audible range of the cabin, should have brought the occupant out to meet us in the fashion common to the wilderness, but no one appeared. We had concluded that the owner could not be far away and decided to wait if we did not find him in, when suddenly we heard a voice from within the cabin call out. There we found Scotty, as he preferred to be called, a half-Indian, half-French trapper. He was in bed with a fractured bone in his leg. While the fracture was not compound, it was bad enough so that Scotty could not get around. He had contrived a splint of sorts but was unable to do much of a job on himself. My previous training in the hospital corps of the Navy came in handy.

Scotty hadn't eaten very well since his accident. (A rotted rung on the ladder up to his smoked-meat cache had broken, dropping him from a hazardous height to the ground.) While Cloud poked up the fire and prepared some food, I went to work on Scotty's leg.

The bone had fortunately not been displaced. It was an obvious fracture. With plaster of paris hundreds of miles away, Scotty's mind was taxed when I asked him if he could remember where we might find some clay as a substitute. We did find some even if it was not the best. Though with reinforcement we made up a fairly good cast.

By the second day at Scotty's cabin we had him in pretty good shape. Plenty of cut wood stacked near his stove, a quantity of food prepared ahead, a pair of improvised crutches crafted for him, and some general putting in order of his cabin, is the way we left him. He would not come along with us to the outside world where he could get help while his bones knit. So successful was the cast, Scotty hobbled on his crutches all the way out to our departure at the water's edge.

A teller of tales—some fantastic, most perhaps remotely feasible—Scotty had Cloud and me joking about their credibility. One story was stranger than the rest. Scotty narrated a tale that had been handed down to him about the Franklin expedition. One member, he said, had escaped death, had deserted the main party, and had lived alone below the arctic circle in the scrub timber.

Historical records that could be pieced together made it quite certain that all of the Franklin party had perished. Yet, could there be a remote chance that records were inconclusive and that one of the party had survived? It would be a great scoop if we could run it down.

The feasibility of the story as it was handed down to Scotty was that this member had deserted the Franklin party early, before the ultimate disaster. Since the command was set up on a military basis, this deserter, according to the tale, dared not make his identity known in any settlement lest he be brought before a military tribunal, tried, and shot. He, therefore, remained in the wilderness, and under an assumed name, traded with the Indians to live as best he could without contacting the outside world. How logical, yet how probably fictional.

Cloud and I laughed off this story along with the rest. But years later as I read more of arctic exploration, that story bothered me. I discussed it with historians who became as intrigued by the tale as I was. Finally, I attempted to look up Cloud, and again make the same canoe journey in order to run down this story if possible. If it proved to be fiction, or failed in substantiation, another canoe journey into that magnificent lake and forest area would be reward enough. In fact, the truth might have been that I was looking for a conventional excuse to make the same voyage again. Furthermore, I had tempted a historian who was sufficiently interested to finance the trip.

What had happened to Cloud in the meantime, the historian and I were not readily able to determine. It seemed that our search for him would be as involved as trying to learn if there actually was a possible survivor of the Franklin party. Ultimately, the so-called grapevine in the Indian country got through to Cloud. He had married and had youngsters, who along with him and his wife were up in the Ontario blueberry country, picking berries. When I found him and suggested that he accompany me and my historian friend on another canoe trip to run down the story about the Franklin deserter, he laughed uproariously and said:

"Did you believe all that B.S.?" I was surprised that in the intervening time, Cloud's English, especially his slang, had become very fluent.

"No," I answered quickly, to save Cloud's confidence in me. "But," I said, "my friend here wants to see if there could possibly be any truth in it. He will pay for the trip and give you good wages besides."

Cloud's answer was classical. "You better damn well believe that story. It's true, sure as hell." A big grin on Cloud's face ended in all three of us winding up with belly laughs. At this point I began to wonder if my historian friend was not just as interested in a canoe trip as he was in the Franklin tale.

We planned the trip for the following open-water season. Cloud agreed to make inquiries in the meantime as to what Indians were trapping in the Far Northern forest area of Scotty's cabin on the nameless lake.

It was too far away. What information we gained was vague and meaningless. The greater difficulty was that if there had been such a deserter, he would now be at an advanced age, well into the nineties, and information, if any, would likely be about him, not from him.

Well equipped, the three of us set off the following season to run down some arctic history that had become mere legend. About ten o'clock one morning weeks later, we pulled into the cove of Scotty's cabin. There was no canoe on the waterfront. A section of the rotting roof had fallen inside. Rain had poured in, creating mildew over the interior's improvised furnishings, wall, and floor. Some of Scotty's possessions remained, but the items that had substantial value were gone. Before we entered the cabin we had an apprehensive feeling that Scotty's bones might be found in the bed if porcupines had not eaten them, but our best analysis of the premises was that Scotty had long been gone. A hundred and fifty miles to the south we came onto a freighting canoe with an elderly Indian, his wife, and two grandchildren. Cloud plied them with a long series of questions in his native tongue, not only about Scotty but about the possible survivor of the Franklin party. Scotty they knew casually. His broken leg had mended and he had even resumed trapping afterward. He had gone to live with a sister on the "outside," they believed. With only the name Scotty, there seemed little chance of learning anything about him on the "outside." As to the possible survivor of the Franklin expedition, the Indians had no knowledge whatever, the answer being a repeated "We don't know." There could possibly have been a deserter from the Franklin expedition. If there was, that secret remains somewhere permanently in the elements of the permafrost, where no tale will tell.

14. Solitude

❦

PEOPLE generally live their lives through in the presence
of others. To be alone, especially in wild regions, for more
than brief periods of time is to most people frustrating. Yet, it
has been quite conclusively established that the cultural measure of a man is his self-sustaining ability to be alone a
generous share of the time. The creative mind especially has
a great need for solitude, or more accurately, isolation in
order to work.

These statements, while seeming rather academic, have special significance, I think, in the examination of the whole question of wilderness aloneness. How gregarious man actually is
by nature, how he develops to the stage where he might be
less gregarious, and how much solitude on the average he
actually can tolerate, hasn't been fully determined. Various
manifestations of loneliness become too complex and only get
one into muddled psychoanalysis. What might be of greater
interest and value, perhaps, is the common reaction of reasonably normal people to aloneness. How much solitude, for ex-

ample, does a person need for gaining such maturity? How much solitude, on the other hand, will it take to impair his mind, if solitude actually can impair his mind?

The term *bushwacky* is a common expression in wilderness regions. It is presumed by many, on not very valid grounds, that an individual isolated too long from others will in time suffer mental disorder. Whatever cases I have seen that might suggest bushwacky tendencies were mental conditions sufficiently inherent in the individual to have caused his state of mind no matter where he chose his environment.

Many trappers I have known lived through winters in the wilderness without human contact of any kind. They have shown no apparent disposition to become bushwacky. Theirs is the long trail, the daily tussle with the elements, arduous treks over snowshoe and canoe routes. In such contests where mistakes are not condoned, man as a rule suffers no mental impairment. His, rather, is a developing mind, the need for hourly challenges and careful calculations that tend more toward increasing maturity.

Before radio and television, trappers especially were known traditionally to be great readers. Men of wisdom write great books, and men who read great books usually develop extraordinary life tendencies.

Solitude has greatly diminished for the trapper and other wilderness dwellers in recent years, of course, with the advent of mechanized mobility. The outboard motor in open water and the snowmobile over snow and ice trails have made access to markets and visits with friends in the outlying regions comparatively routine. The trapper of today is more apt to be concerned with the competitive inroads of synthetic furs than he is with the possible mind-debilitating effects of isolation.

A trapper of my acquaintance whose licensed area is in a region of lakes, rivers, and timber, has periodically bundled up a bale of furs after breakfast, loaded them on a snowmobile, and arrived in a small North Country settlement by dark. After transacting his business and visiting at a friend's home the following day, he would be back at his cabin on the third day in time for a late evening meal. By dog team earlier this trip required two weeks.

Remarking about this modern means of transportation, one might say, "Bully for him." But most trappers would likely disagree as to how "bully" it really is. If the earlier circumstances prevailed, he would prefer the two-week dog-team trip. He can't choose because he is caught up in the competitive fur market. He must dispose of his furs when the prices are at their highest. We are apt to find that the average trapper is a special kind of individual who wouldn't for a moment think that a fine home in the city or suburb, and a paying, confining job or business, would be "worth the candle." Robert Service would likely have described him as "signed and sealed to nature."

A trapper up on the Churchill River was very sad when I visited him a few years ago, in that circumstances had compelled him to sell his dog team, creatures that he loved dearly, in order to compete with a trapping commerce where the snowmobile and radio-reported fur prices had become essential in a fluctuating market.

Here I should hark back to those days when I first met him. He was a fairly young man then. At the time I was interested in seeing the soon-to-come spring caribou migration. Tired from another of many long days of traveling with a dog team, I was prepared to set up camp, when suddenly my dogs became disturbed. They sniffed the air apprehensively and howled. Soon I sensed a faint smell of wood smoke. I thought that it, perhaps, was merely the odor from my Indian smoke-tanned, moosehide mukluks, the smoke odor being so delicate. Presently, off in the distance, I heard just faintly an answering howl, what had to be either a timber wolf or a part-wolf sled-dog. By then, my dogs were getting a bit frantic, focusing their attention down the long stretch of frozen lake.

Days are short in the North Country winter, and there was just enough lingering late twilight to get up the double-walled tent, prepare some food for the dogs, and cook a meal for myself. Once the dogs were fed, they settled down a little, though still uneasy. It was not the kind of uneasiness displayed when a timber wolf howl raised their whole ire, but the kind of anxiety that was typical when nearing a Hudson's Bay Post or settlement.

A three-quarter, or gibbous moon, as it is sometimes called, was just topping the horizon when the dogs finally went into another frenzy. Their heads were set in a single, fixed direction and they tugged violently at their tethering chains. They saw in the dim light something coming down the long sweep of ice that I did not see. Finally, I did see a tiny shadow form on the distant moonlit ice. It turned out to be a man on snowshoes.

A man traveling on snowshoes at night in that vast early wilderness was not to be taken too casually. I donned snow-

The soon-to-come, spring caribou migration still in the scrub forest.

shoes and traveled toward him. He proved to be the trapper in that region. Back at his cabin, he had just perceptibly heard the wolflike, concerted, distant howl of my dogs and was quite sure that it came not from wolves but a dog team. As we met, he shook my hand warmly, pressed my arm, and introduced himself.

"I haven't seen anybody for nearly six months," he said, "it is good to talk to someone. No need to camp out tonight. My cabin is only a few miles down the lake."

The dogs seemed a bit reluctant about being hitched up at that time of night, but as they drew closer to the trapping cabin they could scarcely be held back. I had planned, on entering the caribou migration area, to find some kind of shelter that would be more habitable than my tent to wait out the period before the initial movement of the herd. To accomplish this, I thought that I might even have to rough-in a mini-sized log cabin or move on to the nearest Hudson's Bay Post, days of additional travel beyond the migration route, and return in time for the migration. To find such a warm host in the caribou migration area was way beyond expectations.

We had dog pandemonium when we reached the vicinity of the trapper's cabin. His dogs and mine were ready for a melee, but they couldn't reach one another. He had provided a kennel for his dogs, with a separate area for the occasional isolation of bitches and their litters. Thus, we were able to keep the dogs apart and give my dogs, as well, protection from the cold. Not until the dogs found that they could not get at each other did they settle down enough for the trapper and me to get some sleep. This was not soon, because we talked almost until dawn.

Here, I already judged, was a man of more than ordinary talent and ability to make his way just about anywhere. Nevertheless, he chose to remain in the wilderness during the long winters of the higher latitudes. He could have had human association within a week's sled travel to a post, had he chosen. Rather, for nearly six months he preferred a life where no human voice was heard, for there were no radios at that time, no snowmobiles, no available planes.

Why did he and others do it? The only adequate answer must come from the questioner himself, by experiencing on his own a period of profound wilderness solitude. I doubt the common dictum that a man feels a little ridiculous until he has stood in military battle, but I do not doubt that until a man has lived in solitude for a substantial period, he has little profound existential sense about himself.

I believe that today such solitude should be experienced by every intellectually enterprising individual without the aid of radio or communication of any kind. Once one is removed to wilderness isolation, the outside world, I find, seems rapidly to recede and much of man's exigent concern about a world in stress loses importance. There are moments in the wilderness when an overwhelming feeling is upon one that all human life on earth but oneself no longer exists, and it is this experience of deep subjectiveness that I think man needs later as a complement to properly take his place in society.

My host was up soon after daylight, which in late winter with its brief daylight is not very early. Having talked most of the night, we had slept little. Yet, I felt no imposing drowsiness.

"Take a few more winks," he said, "and I'll have some breakfast going."

Coffee, caribou steak fried in ham fat, and sourdough pancakes; it was all too gastronomically alluring to allow the few extra winks of sleep. Besides, I wanted to see the actual preparation.

Trapping, for him, was largely over for the winter. He had made most of his catch in December before the fur became rubbed and shoddy. His traps had been sprung to prevent any further creatures getting caught. It was an opportune time to visit. We planned to make a trip farther to the north to watch the caribou migration. But there was plenty of time before that, and I greatly enjoyed the interval.

His philosophy of life made me a better listener than I am

generally reputed to be. Perhaps the most significant aspect of it was the mood he had when telling about it, best described as soothing or relaxing. Apprehensions that plague most men seemed farthest from his thoughts. He appeared able to live with his own solutions to life. A voracious reader, a devout learner so to speak, he apparently took much direction from the documented wisdom of the ages. Yet, he treated this wisdom with a kind of intellectual speculation rather than being too much resigned to credence. "After all, every man has to have his own answers," he said.

"Out there under those scrub trees," he pointed out, "are several generations of sled dogs. They came out of the elements of the earth and went back there. Man, by the most honest observation, is no different. He came from the earthy elements and he will, no doubt, return to earth. All the fictional banalities that have been invented to alter that fact do not change the overriding evidence. Conjecture on this score, regardless of its edification, its ritual, lends no contradiction to what every man sees conclusively wherever he is. Nature is a process of germination, growth, and decay. The human mammal tries to exclude himself from this process, but fails utterly in the actuality of the cycle."

Of all this he did not speak disparagingly. To live and return to the earth from which he came, to be a part of its elements, he referred to in a sense as a privilege.

"This," and he swept his hand in a slow, panoramic gesture to indicate the natural world around him, "is a far greater paradise than the illusory nonsense which was invented by early, uninformed scribes."

He was, it might be said, a man who loved the "rocks and rills, the woods and templed hills."

A blizzard tore across the area one day of my visit, starting hours before dawn and continuing through the day. My host aroused me from my deep sleep with breakfast almost ready.

"You are going to have some band music with your breakfast," I heard him say in my half-sleep.

I wondered what this meant, and soon learned. Every interstice of the outside cabin walls became a kind of flute as the wind whistled over it. Windows seemed like drums as the violently gust-driven snow thumped against them. The dogs had crawled into their shelters, now drifted over.

When the storm broke the following morning, calm and sunny, my host was just as expressive.

"Go out there and take a look," he said, "you haven't seen anything like it."

Well, I had, and so had he many times, but the drama of the natural world warrants a thousand replays, none ever dulling. It was a white wilderness of immaculate purity, great knife-edged drifts that caught the early salmon-colored light of dawn. When I went back indoors at my host's call for breakfast, he had an amused smile on his face and said:

"Well, what did you think of it?"

"It seems brand new and better every time," I replied.

To be alive to every living moment, to every phase of weather, to every miracle of the spontaneous, generous earth —this seemed to be his genius. He needed people, but solitude for him did not degrade.

Later we carried packs of camping gear on our backs and moved into an area where the caribou migration was most likely to be seen. The migration, varying from season to season, sometimes en masse but following no special pattern, often is so unpredictable as to leave starvation among the Indians dependent upon the herd to pass in certain areas. Where we now observed them in seemingly countless numbers, moving for three days through the region, can be described only as having been another wonder of the world. Wolves are an integral part of the movement, killing and eating the weak and aged stragglers, thus keeping the vast herd healthy and vigorous.

15. Burning Bridges Behind

WRITERS on outdoor life usually have a substantial reader correspondence. These letters, containing all sorts of inquiries, might at times seem to be excessive extracurricular activity; but by virtue of this correspondence, writers pretty much get to know where they stand with the reading public. Letters can and often do become a kind of private book review. Like the doctor and the lawyer, the writer gets an insight into the life of his clientele. Perhaps the most intriguing letters I receive come from those who want to burn their urban and social bridges behind, and take up life in the wilderness—the "get-away-from-it-all" element comprising several age brackets.

There was a time when this escape idea was highly individualized. The rare, intrepid individual simply took off unceremoniously on his semihermitage and shacked up somewhere away from the madding crowd. If he succeeded in his isolation, which was not often wholly realized, his identity along the back trail of life usually faded. On some occasions he has been sought by lawyers who would bestow upon him sums of money, sometimes veritable fortunes, through inheritance; but owing to his not having been previously apprised of his position as a possible heir, his inheritance would wind up in the public coffers.

A great many letters of late have come from those who have joined the ranks of the Hippy element in the United States and those who would like to take up residence in the wilds of Canada, some apparently to escape the draft. Then there are the few who in all sincerity desire to seek life with a little repose in it, away from the deterioration of a polluted, industrially obsessed world.

The very young, in general, who are primarily interested in outdoor life—those whose letters appear to be written with stubby pencils on which they bear down hard on the pages of a Five & Dime Store tablet—to them I try to give whatever encouragement I am able, on the theory that here may lie special potentials for good.

Letters come from leaders who would start wilderness communes. Usually their plan is impracticably idyllic. Somewhere far away from the cities, they suggest that there must be areas in the wilds where nature offers benevolence. Every citizen of the commune must qualify, they explain, as an individual who "seeks humanistic values rather than monetary ones." There, in some wilderness Shangri-la, they believe, the commune population will "thrive in high principle, wholly cooperative, directly opposite to the confusing problems of the great urban centers." *Love* is the central theme. "Hate and disregard shall be unknown." Ah me, if only it could be so!

There is no hint in the proposed commune of organization, subsistence levels, the needed performance of many undesirable tasks; the list carries on and on. I never get to know what would happen if one individual came to hate another fiercely for no more logical reason than the way he holds his fork when he eats. Settling of a substantial population in any area fails to consider that inevitably it will take on most pit-falls of urban society by the need to carry on the simple physical functions of daily life and its consequent disposal problems.

The idealistic road of life for the young invariably forks. Before one comes to the fork there are a great many mixed emotions and thoughts about sex, romance, mating, single-blessedness, adventure, accumulation of means or merely sub-sistence means, leisure, freedom of the spirit, and so on, in the insecure saddle of every horse on the complex merry-go-round of life.

Plenty of time, idealistic youth feels, is available to plan and partake of advantages along the route. Suddenly that realistic human fork in the road appears. One branch of departure says that this is the road to take: the high road of romance, the road to adventure, leisure, individual purpose. If a person has the faculty for taking this road, he is rare indeed. The chances are that human nature has dictated otherwise. Too often it will be the conventional road—one of the girl, children, the job, the pretentious home, the two-car garage, the cocktail bar, and the two registered purebred dogs, or some slight urban modification of this.

Caught in the conventional life, the aspirant toward the idyllic has yet not given up on the hope of adventure into high places. Once married, he will "take along the little pal" on his wilderness jaunts. She has convinced him that she "loves the outdoors." But it is likely that the closest she has come so far, on her own initiative, to the grandeur of nature is adoring the shop flowers brought to her on those special oc-casions. If she belongs to that overwhelming typical majority to which I refer, the moment she has caught the first recipro-cal twinkle in the male eye across the room, she is laying plans to feather her nest. The next phase will be to laud whatever interest the male has. If that interest is the wilderness, she will manifest a strong affinity for hiking, packhorse and canoe trails, sailing the high seas, etc. This will continue even into the first and part of the second wilderness trip. A siege of cold, rainy weather too often will stamp her disapproval on the whole wilderness program. It will not be outright, but diverting and femininely subtle. Suggestion will likely be made to rent a cabin and make sallies, to avoid camping out. When the first baby arrives, the damping down of wilderness adventure will have lost its original subtle approach to domestic mandates.

But not, I hasten to add, in every instance of feminine proclivity.

A great university through exhaustive research concluded that only one human being out of every fifty thousand expressed significant perception of nature, especially any profound approach to natural phenomena. Perhaps the statistic may go wrong here and there, though it will not be far from the conventional pattern. At least, it will suggest the need for being highly selective where the choice of a wilderness companion is concerned. Clues to his or her identity as being sincerely interested in the wilderness will be indicated by a personal, not prompted, affinity for natural interests. The mistake most often made is the belief that initiation into any activity is all that is required. When you consider that few have a devout interest in the wilderness, the pattern becomes clearer. For example, many men—and fewer women—hunt, but beyond this manifest little interest in natural values. They go afield to destroy with a gun what wildlife they can and hurry back almost in panic once their bag limit has been reached. The wilderness song is not very vocal in their life.

It might seem to the reader that we have strayed from the topic of this chapter. Not at all. The individual who seeks to burn his urban bridges behind him must be a distinct kind of individual, male or female, whose interest in wilderness pursuits is on a par with that of the individual whose passion for art, or any other profound interest, is so great, frustration is suffered when that interest cannot be pursued.

There seems to be one important factor scarcely ever considered by the "bridge burners" who write to me. Seldom do they bring into emphasis a pursuit that will enable them to maintain an interest once they have settled in their wilderness sanctuary. Those who have hunting and fishing as the chief interest are always, and I emphasize *always*, destined to failure, though at the outset they believe implicitly that such interest will be amply sustaining.

More determining is the matter of income. In earlier days when living standards were not so luxurious, austerity played less of a role than it does today. To accept the wilderness on its most elemental terms, and at the same time attempt to apply the inflationary living standards of urban life today, is to court failure at the start, unless one has capital. This, by its own pecuniary attraction, too often keeps the affluent individual conventionally straightjacketed and confined to the city.

I do, however, know a man who has succeeded in accepting the wilderness in its most elementary sense on the modern inflationary basis, but he did it by having discovered a mineral deposit while living in the Canadian wilderness, and selling his interest to a mining company. If ever an individual was not influenced by the sudden accumulation of wealth, it is he. I attribute this to his already developed, indigenous wilderness life. He suffers no apparent passion for materialism. Since he dislikes the incursion of the plane on the wilderness, he prefers to have his provisions and supplies brought in by two Indians over several days of water and portage trails, or by dog sled in winter. This is highly agreeable to the Indians in that it provides them with daily wages.

The cabin of this prospector is a masterpiece of log work. Being a highly skilled axman, he insisted upon fitting the logs and doing all of the technical construction himself, though he employed three Indians to cut the logs from the forest and peel them.

A fourth Indian was a cook. What amused me as I saw the cabin rise on its foundation was that there was not enough work for three strong Indians, and scarcely enough work for a full-time cook. Once the ax work started, there really wasn't much for the Indians to do until the log was notched out at both ends and simulated the pattern of the log below it for fit. The Indians did what they do quite well—they relaxed. Contrary to the perversions of white men desperately trying to exalt their own race, Indians are not, as accused, lazy. But this does not mean that they also tend to carry on the perpetual industrial frenzy of the white man. When the intervals between hoisting a log into place came, or turning it over for scribing or notching, the Indians at first seemed a bit apprehensive about standing around doing nothing. When they asked what they could do in these intervals, they were told, "Try sitting."

There were rainy days when construction of the cabin was interrupted. There also were days when the Indians he had hired fished, hunted, and gathered wild rice. It didn't seem to matter much. Their daily wages went on just the same. I thought of a famous early saying, "If you have but one dollar and you must spend it, spend it as though it were a leaf and you were the owner of boundless forests." The man who hired these Indians was relatively as generous before he gained the fortune from his mineral discovery as he was afterward, though initially he had only a pension on which to live. To have the boundless forest, it is much easier to spend the leaf, but too often one sees the grudging "sacrifice" of the leaf by the boundless owner.

It seems quite impossible to consider the so-called escape concept without examining man's individual capability for isolating himself from society. He is by temperament just as likely in most cases to become at odds with isolation as he is at odds with the attrition of society upon his nerves. The middle road on any approach to life might appear easier and the safer way, but then one suffers that taunting indictment of failing to make bold excursions at both ends of life's adventure spectrum, choosing only the insipid middle course.

Never in the half dozen decades of my life have I seen such

a great trend toward making some kind of escape as that
which dominates modern society. It is manifested partly in the
euphoric drugs that have created a national catastrophe. It is
most evident in the diminishing respect that youth has for the
obsessions of industry and business. Where once these were a
kind of success utopia to strive for, much of our youth now
fails to see them as sufficient in the search for life's fulfillment.

What strikes me as confusing in the new tendency for detachment from the establishment is that the detachment is generally more apparent than real. The young element that boasts
a detachment from the establishment and merely wanders aim-
lessly through the cities and along highways suggests the
"independence" of the leech. In short, they seem as addicted
to urbanity as though they held the establishment closest to
their ultimate choice of a viable existence. In my travels through
the wilderness or semi-remote areas, I see little of this element—the most logical sanctuary, one might presume, for
escape.

Interrogating these young people to glean from them at
least a hint of a philosophical basis for having chosen their
pseudo-detachment, I find that largely there is no substantial,
constructive qualification given by them above mere resent-
ment of established society. When in my younger days I
used up only the most "undesirable" weather parts of the year
to garner subsistence and leisure for the whole year, I saw no
objection to making an honest compromise with the establishment.

Euphoria—"an often unaccountable feeling of well-being
or elation"—this is what the escapist no less than the narcotic
addict apparently tries to achieve. For a short time the addict
achieves this with drugs. Then, as we have seen, he pays for it
with long stretches of agonizing reaction.

Is it possible to achieve this "often unaccountable feeling of
well-being or elation," the so-called euphoria, without de-
structive drugs? We might try to answer that. All reasonably
healthy people do enjoy to some degree, no doubt, moments

of elation, regardless of what the interest, the environment, or the circumstance. What we need to determine is, Under what conditions does an individual have the most consistently occurring feeling of such well-being?

Since some seventy percent of our population has rushed to the city, intent upon acquiring something there and hoping to escape from what they left behind, the question arises, Did they find that feeling of well-being in the city? Or did they leave the best hope for it behind? In a manner of speaking, they obviously not only burned their bridges behind, they reached a point of no return by a form of insidious urban captivity—the placing of themselves in a position of *inescapable, excessive need.*

Material want looms most important in the first half of adult life. It does not diminish rapidly in the second half, but it surely tapers off. There comes a time when neither the storage nor utility of many material things is compatible with well-being. Empty space on a shelf, literally and figuratively, later in life has a greater attraction than saturated storage capacity—one starts giving things away and enjoying the luxury of riddance.

Too many toys cause a dulling satiation in a child. In adulthood gadgets are no less satiating, but they have the added woe that every additional toy or item of utility encumbers the mind as well as its respective storage place. Urban life, largely devoid of natural interest and slanted to artifice and mechanized utility, inevitably becomes a gadget-obsessed existence.

There never can come a time when the material purge is entirely successful, of course. But there can come a time when the deletion process of accumulation becomes easier.

Giving up things might seem to imply a program of desertion, a shirking of responsibility. Here one can afford to be arrogant. When in my own case urban life reached a point of inviability, I simply abandoned it for natural regions where life proved more viable. When after a fair share of affluence I found myself anxiously checking market reports every day, I dumped the fluctuating investments which were the object of my concern, and bought government bonds. The unburdening of mind-absorbing encumbrances opened a new outlook. I became more interested in seeing the sun come over the mountain peaks, more satisfied to sit relaxed and watch wild-life, more content to earn a dollar from my writing than a thousand in a sharp real estate transaction. As the literal dumping of many material things corrected a dull-care concern over them, I discovered the difference between the words *price* and *value*.

Euphoria—a feeling of well-being or elation? Yes, but not unaccountable. It comes when the body and the mind are in tune with a more reposeful existence. It comes when one sees morning break over a natural world. It comes when one can observe a pair of otter moving down the lake, playing with each other as they swim, or when listening to a hermit thrush singing in the backwoods just before dusk. It comes especially, I find, when the focus turns toward a humanistic and natural world. But I hasten to add that this turning is not a spontaneous act; it is the careful orientation of mind, a diverting process from that which fails to ennoble, and an adherence to that which refreshes and inspires.

16. Nostalgia

WHATEVER the present or future holds, there appears to be no full compensation in the present at least, and much uncertainty in the foreseeable future, that will make up for losses of past wilderness values. We can suppose that much of this is illusory, but if so, it is to many people, nevertheless, very real. Reasoning away sentiment is ineffective when sentimental yearning has no possible means of gratification. Yearning for some past irrecoverable wilderness condition can become a malady so depressing to some that those suffering from it are frustrated to the point of psychosis. Material advantage beyond any possible contingency gives them little compensatory solace.

We can pass this off as nonsensical wistfulness which intellectual maturing ought to dispel, but the strange aspect of the whole psychological problem is that all of us, at one time or another, suffer nostalgia in some degree. Women suffer anguish when they lose that heightened bloom of youth. Actresses who depend on this early bloom and lose it have a high suicide rate. Athletes who have been celebrated for their great events often suffer despondency when they no longer can accomplish the physical feats of their prime. Is it unusual then that some of us suffer excruciatingly when the most endearing aspect of life—a natural, inspiring environment—is hopelessly ravaged?

One cannot quite determine whether it was the inspirational and impressionable nature of youth or the more natural early conditions which tend to hang so wistfully in memory. I suppose there is really no categorical separating of the two. I have tried to recapture the early-day thoughts that occupied my mind as I sat expectantly waiting for a train in a rail station, a loaded packsack of camp equipment and provisions at my side—the first lap likely to Winnipeg, Manitoba, with the final destination some remote "jumping off place" in the then inviolate Canadian wilderness.

Winnipeg, a centrally located gate to the wild country, has the outpost department of the Hudson's Bay Company. There one picked up such equipment as Indian-made snowshoes, moosehide moccasins, and other items highly integral with the remote wilderness life—articles not available in the average sporting goods, hardware, or clothing store. At the outpost supply house of the Hudson's Bay Company you did not saunter up to a clerk and tell him your needs as you did in a retail store. You were cordially greeted by a clerk, and when your needs were expressed, you were ushered into an inner office for a visit with an officer of "The Company," where your inquiry for whatever items you required gained importance. No less did your destination become important to "The Company." A Hudson's Bay Post in the interior that might happen to be on your wilderness itinerary would have a factor (manager), you were told, who would be glad to see you. You must spend a few days with him as a guest. He would have no news other than what you and some chance wilderness traveler, or the supply-canoe brigade, would bring in for him, for then there were no radio communications, no planes, no outboard motors, no snowmobiles to bring him messages. Thus, your arrival at the Hudson's Bay Company outpost store division took on special meaning and purpose.

A now second-rate hotel in Winnipeg—then a leading one —was the stopping place of most who were headed into the wilderness. In the clothes closets were important names scribbled on the plastered walls. They made little impression on me in those early days due to my limited knowledge of wilderness exploration history. Somehow the names and accompanying notations lingered vaguely in memory and were recalled later as I began to read the actual exploits of these adventurers into far-off places.

One day I talked about them to a man of considerable means in the United States, whose interest was in the collecting of manuscripts, art treasures, and historical pieces. From our meeting in Minneapolis we proceeded to Winnipeg in search of the inscribed names, and especially to recover, if possible, the early guest registers. He would, he said, have the plastered sections of the closet carefully removed and crated for later exhibition. But our trip was in vain. The very old, dusty, time-browned pages of the registers had been thrown into the furnace when new owners took charge, the signatures and notations on the closet walls painted over. When my friend told the hotel owners that he would have paid handsomely for the priceless inscriptions and the registers, they had a look of despondency which I thought deeper than regret. It seems that a sense of values can never be equated with cost.

Recollections of the past have a way of diminishing in importance, or just as likely becoming intensified with the years. I believe it was Clarence Darrow who recalled with deep emotion those childhood days when he went sliding on a sled with his companions down the hill behind his home. In adult life he visited this childhood home, especially intent upon seeing the hill which had left such a lasting impression. The hill proved to be a mere mound where as a child he could not have slid but a few yards at most.

While we tend to magnify the values we place on early things, we should not overlook the fact that the very essence of interest any time in life depends on our ability to intensify, exalt and glorify. There can be a wide range between the individual who looks upon the natural scene with a myopic eye and the author of the famed lyrics of "America," for example, who was inspired to write, "I love Thy rocks and rills, Thy woods and templed hills; My heart with rapture thrills. . . ."

When I left the Hudson's Bay Company outpost department with my outfit now complete, ready to head into the wilderness, I was in those days treading with ecstatic, youthful steps. A misty rain was falling on the streets of Winnipeg as I sought a restaurant. This adversity of weather could have no possible deleterious effect on me whatever. It seemed integral and right—just another atmospheric mood. Patrons in the restaurant showed a novel interest in my rain shirt and sou'wester rain hat. There were sympathetic smiles from the diners, as though they had now seen the best solution for their outwitting rain.

I had made arrangements with the Hudson's Bay Company to rent a canoe at one of the outposts and had been given a letter of credit for various outpost purchases. Thus for the moment, as I prepared to eat my dinner, I lived in the enchantment of a mind rich in anticipation. The next train for the North was scheduled to leave many hours later, so I dined in great leisure. The restaurant being a bit crowded at high noon, I shared a table with a man who proved to be a Winnipeg physician. He took an intense vicarious interest in my planned solo journey into the wilds. After dinner he invited me to his office and provided several adjuncts to my simple first-aid kit, along with instructions for their use. In the interior, they proved of great value, not for me but for some Indians I met who had sustained various injuries and infections.

Nine Indian families, I learned from the Hudson's Bay Company official, were encamped on a rather large island in Tetu Lake. As I approached the island in my canoe, I saw only some boys less than teen-age and a woman on the waterfront. The boys eagerly lifted the canoe upon the shore and stowed my pack underneath the overturned canoe. I was told that most of the men were net fishing at the upper end of the lake, others having gone hunting for several days.

I shall never forget the grandeur of the woman as she stood well up on the rockbound shore silhouetted against the blue sky. She wore a red bandanna handkerchief on her head, had on a brightly colored calico dress and wrap-around, beaded moosehide moccasins. While she spoke no English and I no Cree, this was no handicap since two of the boys had been off to a mission school during the winter months, I learned, and they translated my inquiries with a few additional flourishes of their own, which left me out of some obvious humor that crept into the translation. Both boys and the Indian woman seemed highly amused at whatever I said. When I made it clear that I would like to visit for a few days if possible, there was added amusement, which confused me as to my welcome. I learned that the crux of the whole joke rested on what the Indian woman, who had a marvelous sense of humor, had told the boys. It was simply that it was a big island, that I was among friends, that a few days could not amount to much to a man as young as I, and that once the girls on the island saw me I would not be able or even want to leave.

I asked if I should wait until some of the men returned to learn if it was alright for me to stay on. The answer came soon and with brevity. The men would be glad to have me stay, besides—and one of the boys pointed toward the woman —"She is the boss."

This is not unusual. Women among the Indians have often had the effect of strong matriarchal influence.

A long day with the paddle and several portages had left me

both hungry and tired. Uppermost was the need to pitch my light sailcloth wedge tent and prepare a meal. The best place seemed to be a spot well removed from the various Indian shelters, which were scattered down through the island. Once my tent was pitched, I soon had tea water going and a bannock propped up in a frypan before a brisk fire.

The boys, apparently finding my presence a new source of interest, raced back and forth from their own camp to mine, obviously transmitting every detail of my actions, including my offer of candy. When I began eating the bannock and drinking my tea, one of the lads was off like a streak, returning soon with some cooked moose meat. At first I had suspicions that authority was not behind the giving, but this notion was allayed when the Indian lads insisted that one had to have meat with bannock and that "she" had told them to be quickly off with the meat before I got the bannock swallowed.

Having in a sense intruded on these people, it seemed prudent on second thought to give whatever indication I could to the Indian lads that I might be moving on after a brief visit. Since I had first asked to visit a few days, this had in it a note of contradiction which apparently was conveyed to the men when several of them returned that evening from the upper-lake fishing trip. At my invitation they gathered around my fire. More meat was brought from the main Indian camp. I supplied the bannock and tea, making it a rather festive kind of bannock with raisins, dried whole milk, and additional sugar.

The youngest of the men had a fair understanding of English, which enabled all of us through his interpretation to exchange views and ideas. Perhaps my being alone had something to do with their ready acceptance of my visit. Traveling alone somehow seems to point up one's wilderness competence. The Hudson's Bay Company insignia on the canoe I had rented might have suggested to them that I could in some official capacity be with "The Company." In any event, the men made it plain that I should stay as long as I chose. I had brought tobacco for them and bags of white beads, needles and thread for the women, which warmed their attitudes. White beads seemed to be preferred to the colored, another bit of information I had gleaned during my visit at the Hudson's Bay Company.

Early the next morning I was invited to join the men going to the upper end of the lake to pick their whitefish nets. Since it is generally regarded that the paddler in the stern has a demonstrated superiority with a paddle, I stood amidship, as it were, beside my canoe, and by the act of mild suggestion while facing the stern, indicated that my partner should assume that position.

With a strong wind, we were soon pitching through a sea of whitecaps. It was not possible to watch the canoe strokes of my partner, though I felt a power and direction in the progress of the craft that was reassuring. I could, of course, observe every action of those in the other two canoes, the angle of their bodies, the arm positions, the length of the paddle strokes—which, surprisingly, I found to be rather short. The logic of these short paddle strokes quickly became apparent. Once the paddle thrust had been made for the forward motion of the canoe, there was less resistance to the water in the upward retrieve of the paddle for the next stroke.

While it gave me no particular concern, I did wonder what the noonday meal would be at the upper end of the lake. Seeing the Indians with no "packed lunch," I followed suit and assumed that if they could practice a Spartan existence and go without eating until evening, I could do the same. The long paddle to the far end of the lake against a sea kicking up spray-blown waves suggested what a Finlander once proclaimed when he was not being well fed on a job, "You can't run steam engine on newspaper."

The skill with which the Indians pulled in behind every windbreak point, even crossing the lake at times to get behind long stretches of mainland and island-protective shore, made it obvious to me that my wilderness canoe-travel education, if not actually initiated, was being upgraded.

Previous to that time I had not seen fishing nets used. Picking fish out of nets from the bow seat of the canoe while the paddler in the stern keeps the canoe on a course in rough water is more of an art than I had assumed. I undertook to paddle the canoe, and while my paddling style was that of the white man, my control of the canoe was apparently adequate, for the Indians sought to praise my efforts, and to accuse an Indian of insincerity in his praise would be not to know the Indian.

When we had picked the nets, the day was getting past noon. I had daydreams of boiled rice and moose meat, of brown-crusted bannock with slathers of camp-made apricot jam on it, of great draughts of tea. As my dreams turned into mere hallucinations of appetite and no food, I suddenly looked up and saw two of the Indians going ashore. With no lost motion, they soon had large, long-blackened cooking pails suspended over a fire.

When we had left the island early in the morning, there were neither cooking pails nor food in any of the canoes—giving no promise that we would eat until our return. It was simply that the pails had been left hanging in the forest near the fishing area, from previous trips to the nets.

A kind of merriment prevailed around the cook fire, but I saw no food, though food there was. One of the Indians carried a number of whitefish strung on a stick to the campfire, and once the large cooking pail of water was boiling full tilt, in went a handful of salt and the fish. In a second pot went a handful of tea, taken from a buckskin pouch.

Food. And drink. In that mealtime episode I was to learn what probably was the most elemental, the simplest, approach to sustaining human beings down through a vast history of primitive life. Here I found no condiment embellishments, no need to pamper appetites, no fussy discrimination of taste, no dishes except tin cups rather ingeniously made with finger-grips from discarded food tins. When the fish were boiled, each of us went to the pot with a sharpened stick and, as it were, fished out a fish. Off came the skin from the fish with a simple flip of the thumb, the point being to eat the fish as one would corn on the cob. All of us chatted and laughed, for here, despite its elemental simplicity, was a festive occasion. I could visualize, in fine hotel restaurants, tables set with sterling and linen, with champagne bottles swaddled in cloth napkins in tubs of ice, pheasant served under silver covers, and coffee poured from fancy urns. By comparison, such luxury would have seemed like sophisticated nonsense at the time, for here among these Indians was a form of epicurism, if one can assume that hearty appetites and taste have reached quintessence.

I was hungry and I ate. I ate until I felt almost an abdominal distension. A few gulls bobbed on the water in front of us, then came more gulls, by some communication puzzle I have never been able to solve. They knew what would be forthcoming, the parts of the whitefish that man did not eat. Is there a more delicious fish in the world than the whitefish from cold Northern waters, especially when optimum health and vigor set the table?

I had the feeling of being observed, though this was not apparent. I tried to imitate as closely as possible every action of the Indians. Obviously, they saw this, but at no moment did they in the least seem to regard me as alien to their circle, to their own way of life. If I failed to hold my fish correctly to get every succulent morsel from it, I was not at all in the embarrassing position of the fellow attending his first formal dinner, confused as to the proper use of an array of silverware.

In time, as I came to know these people more intimately, I broached the subject of the white man's compatibility with the Indian culture. No doubt, I moved, sat, and walked differently from the Indian. I know now that we utterly fail to make full adjustment to the wilderness that is an Indian's development from childhood, and to an extent inherent. I was the product of an entirely different environment—wholly another culture. I was trying in the short space of time to alter habits ingrown for centuries, perhaps, in the reshaping of reflexes that could never reach that development of long wilderness life gained from heritage to heritage.

There is a delightful repose in the whole manner of the wilderness Indian. I soon came to respect their way of life and later to yearn deeply for their company. For them there were no panic buttons to press. They lived as though an eternity lay before them, and because of this it seemed that the natural world always stood still long enough for them to go aboard.

One might hope that such people could go on forever recreating their culture. But this was not to be. Most of those I knew and held dear have grown old and are now gone. Their sense of values, not passed on, went with them. The young are reaching for that which, as it does to most of us, too often leads to frustration.

Yet, I have recently observed a new trend. Indians, as well as other ethnically oppressed people, are demanding that their cultures be at least respected. While the Indian culture will likely not be assimilated in our frenzied society, it might suggest the advantage of much needed repose. We can afford to slow down long enough to allow the more profound values of life to catch up with us.

17. The Wilderness Tomorrow

A KIND OF pilgrimage reaches me. Largely it is the young with an eye to outdoor life who look, if not with despair, then with apprehension on their hopes for the future. But there are others, the older adults who try ecologically for realization of a better life now and for their remaining years. With three-score-and-ten years well behind me as a criterion on which to gauge the future, what can I tell them? Are the years of wilderness enjoyment ahead too inscrutable? Should I presume with an optimistic hypothesis that all will work itself out?

The answers have to be as inaccessibly far-reaching as the questions. Perhaps the mistake most of us make about the present and future wilderness is that we tend to regard it only in its age-old pristine state.

A rather paradoxical concept—one which in essence, I think, has a great deal of merit—is that all the world, no matter how developed, no matter how urbanized and ravaged, is still potentially wilderness. This may seem a bit obscure until we examine it. The general idea expounded here is that natural laws dominate all of the world, and only man's *continual* irruption of its surface by construction keeps it from reverting in time to a wholly natural state again. *Continual* has to be emphasized in this concept. We discover this in the word *maintenance*. The moment a building or other structure has been erected above ground, no matter how seemingly impervious it is to weather, the natural elements start disintegrating it. Bridges are painted perpetually; when finished, the crews go to the opposite ends and start painting them again. If man paused momentarily in his industrial endeavor—that is, a moment considered relative to the infinity of time, or even a reasonably protracted period of time—every boasted structure on the face of the earth would from disintegration fall back into soil, to implement natural growth. Note the accompanying illustration of an abandoned asphalt highway being reduced to soil by the effect of frost upheaval, decay, and growth in just nineteen years. Many of the hotels and office buildings erected in my childhood are already obsolete, no less are they eroded and currently being razed to be replaced by new structures: replacement, replacement ad infinitum. Unless replacement were incessant, the world would eventually flower everywhere without a single artificial edifice in existence.

Is it not possible, therefore, that with this ephemeral nature of material things and the short life of existing neglectful populations, the future might hold out a completely nature-revised world for generations yet unborn? Surely the natural laws will persevere.

As a writer on wilderness themes, my life has been, and for a time will probably continue to be, closely allied with natural phenomena. An urban life has to be considered different only in a conventional sense. We are all products of nature, destined to be controlled, and in time eliminated, by the same natural laws.

What is this persevering, ever-pervading nature? If an important aspect of it always has been, is, and will continue to

". . . an abandoned asphalt highway being reduced to soil . . . in just nineteen years."

be, growth and decay, is this ever-continuing and repeating growth and decay not as evident in the pretentious or modest urban house rotting down in time as it is evident in the prostrate trunk of a postmature and fallen wilderness tree going into humus? Obviously, what I am trying to point out here in principle is that man's greatest effort to "develop" the wilderness—that is, his struggle to replace the wilderness now and in the future with utilitarian needs—is and will be at its most optimum achievement only a temporary incursion upon the earth's surface, a feeble opposition timewise to the natural forces. Industrial development on the land can in the infinity of time, thus, be only a momentary skirmish in the final war against the natural elements, the winning of which inevitably has to be that of nature's reversion process, not man's temporary incursive enterprise. There may be a moral here in the relentless, futile grasping for ephemeral material things.

In the "pilgrimage" to which I alluded earlier, I seem to be the object of considerable disappointment to those who visit me. Here on the St. Croix River, less than an hour's drive from the dense metropolitan populations of Minneapolis and St. Paul, life gains a certain repose, it being comfortably removed from the madding crowd, as it were, in a setting of hardwood and coniferous forest, with a view over a mile-wide valley. It presupposes for the visiting metropolitan citizen a semiwilderness retreat of sorts. Having read my books on the wilderness, my urban visitors often have conjured up wilderness images, probably expecting to see in my residence something comparable to a wildlife-oriented curio display. Surely, they presume, there must be animal skins hanging on my walls; a library limited to the adventures of a "savage" wilderness; pertinent wilderness gear stowed about; furniture contrived from the raw, bark-covered trunks of diamond willow and other woods; even the stuffed heads of wild animals (forgive me, head hunters) hung insanely, as if their noggins were curiously protruding through my walls to see what was going on domestically. Some visitors assume that I use kerosene lamps or candles for light, and I have on occasion had messages and telegrams brought to my door, on the assumption that certainly I could not be reached by so modern an invention as the telephone. It is this concept that the average wilderness devotee presumes to find now and hopes to project into the future in his wilderness idealism.

The pristine disillusionment of these visitors is quite complete on their arrival. They find my residence to be a house of quarried stone rather than one of logs. And if it is more substantially built than the conventional dwelling, it is only because I built it with my own hands. When the entrance-way is flooded with electric light for their arrival, they appear to experience another disappointment. Once inside, their eye is caught by the flame of a fireplace which momentarily raises their hope. This hope drops when they find that the house is not heated by the fireplace but electrically, the kitchen also electrified, the fireplace having been provided just for cheer. If their next gaze shifts to furniture, they unhappily see some "period" pieces, and an imported hand-carved walnut dining room set, along with a few pieces of furniture made by me with power tools from select kinds of wood purchased at modern lumber yards. As they peruse my library, their disillusionment becomes more apparent when the "savage" wilderness fiction is absent. Books on art, music, literature of the ages, science, philosophy, celestial navigation, books of reference, and as many general subjects as diversified interest in life will allow, form the modest library of about a thousand volumes. None of this sophistication of living, they think, can possibly be equated with a natural life pursuit; and yet, all of it is elementarily as much a part of nature's phenomena as the vegetation that grows around the premises.

Curiously my visitors want to know what has happened to the wilderness approach that emanates from my books. Thus, a kind of fictional fancy is their conjectured wilderness. And yet, the various subjects contained in the more or less thousand volumes, by almost as many authors, show the origin of their material to be based largely on some deriving factor of natural phenomena.

Visitors in the majority—and I note the exception—do not want to hear that I travel through the wildest areas of the continent with compass and celestial navigation. They would rather believe that I have some special talent for finding my way instinctively—a faculty that science has conclusively proved no one possesses.

Our present concept of wilderness and that of the future, should thus lie not in the primitive, but in an understanding of the natural laws that govern and shape the universe. We can never gain this understanding unless we regard as best we can the whole scope of the earth's natural operative forces. We can, of course, study natural laws firsthand in the pristine state of a wilderness setting in order to derive an understanding of how these laws basically operate. We can also study them in the metropolis and in the laboratory, or examine them there to see how ghastly the consequences are when these natural laws are perverted by excessive artifice—man floundering out of his proper environment as so much of life in big cities today testifies.

Nevertheless, in all fairness, we have to say that man among the rational element is becoming more ecologically conscious about the prospect of tomorrow's wilderness. I have noticed, along with this later revaluation of wilderness, a desperate parallel effort to salvage the values of the past as well in many respects. The shortage of early originals in furniture, guns, hand-powered devices, and a number of things has prompted manufacturers to simulate originals for popular sale. The past shunned has become the past revered. We have observed in such organizations as the Sierra Club, the National Audubon Society, and the National Wildlife Federation, growing forces to preserve the remaining wilderness areas; in fact, even a serious effort has been made to re-create wilderness areas on the tailings of open-pit mining operations and other industrially ravaged areas. Legislation, though tragically slow, nevertheless tends to be working in this direction for enhancing conservation projects, especially for future micro-wilderness area development.

There is, however, still a continuing yet unstemmed conflict between the encroaching mechanical world, its populations, and the world of inviolate nature. But the fanaticism of mechanization has fortunately at last found some figurative wrenches thrown into its machinery. Snowmobile owners in their zeal to run rampant over every stretch of snow-covered ground—parks, farms, wilderness areas, and roads—now are being confined by local, state, and federal legislation. If we can make a prediction, that confinement will relegate the owner-ability of the snowmobile to a highly restricted one—to its proper use, avoiding much of rampant abuse. The airplane has already been caught in much the same squeeze, banned from National Forests where its obtrusion became a menace to the preservation of future wilderness values. We have seen industry, in a few instances by intelligent choice but largely by legislative demand, cutting back on its ecological depredations. Rivers are being experimentally cleaned up.

Those who expected to find, in a near-city, suburban area, skins or stuffed animal heads on my walls, candles and a wood-burning stove, were, I venture to say, perverting the wilderness concept as incongruously as those who impose a complex modernization on a remote wilderness. It is, I repeat, simply a matter of propriety. One does not pitch a tent alongside a hotel. As I have explained elsewhere, in the two wilderness cabins which my wife and I own and occupy in the Canadian wilderness, modernity of domestic equipment is drastically reduced, not because of any inherent aversion to the modern, but simply because practicability of appliances ceases when complication of service and maintenance seriously detracts from wilderness life. City, suburbia, and wilderness—to each its own.

The wilderness tomorrow will likely continue to be enjoyed by the same deletion process of cumbersomeness in equipment that it is now and has been down through the centuries.

The future wilderness, of course, will survive only by the nonincursion of artificial elements. Where wilderness is concerned, we need to consider *development* synonymous with *vandalism*.

That the attitude toward the wilderness will enjoy a gradually increasing sophistication and consequent hands-off protection, I now fully believe. That our greatest motives spring from a better knowledge of natural phenomena is becoming more and more apparent. The old concept of the wilderness, that it is something to ravage for profit alone, is diminishing, though the idea dies stubbornly. That the wilderness on which man has long turned his back has now become a source for great scientific and aesthetic study is unquestionably evident. But most significant—we have discovered that wilderness is absolutely indispensable for future human survival at all.

That we have yet a long way to go in resolving the preservation of tomorrow's wilderness is demonstrated by some strange violations of late. Zoos have to keep all-night vigilance to prevent a certain, not small, subnormal element from destroying the wild animals, a situation which psychologists believe stems from a carry-over, innate fear of the wild. Recently, some young men in their twenties tried to harass a polar bear in a St. Paul, Minnesota, zoo. The animal had earlier been made partly blind from rocks hurled by teen-agers and some older youths. In the recent case, one of the lads trying to plague it accidentally slipped on some ice and fell into the pit. Since the bear was seriously clawing the young man, it had to be shot to save his life. Perhaps there was some just punishment in the lad's fright and injury, but the court viewed this case of wildlife vandalism as of little consequence, if we are to consider the lenient penalty that was meted out. It seems that even the law lacks understanding and respect for wilderness values. High, costly fences, instead of sounder judicial sense, now have to be thrown around zoos, along with an increased number of just as costly police guards, to prevent a stupid and vicious segment of the populace from destroying the wildlife —what they believe to be their "natural enemy," and what they consider it their unquestioned prerogative to destroy. Man's fear of wild animals is traditional, perhaps one of the greatest nonsensical fears throughout man's history. We lose our pseudo-fears and superstitions slowly, and too generally, seldom gain a sense of values.

A vast revision of our game, timber-cutting, and mining laws will, of course, also have to enter into the preservation of tomorrow's wilderness. The loose rhetoric that goes with the methods used in "harvesting" our wildlife and timber is just as absurd here as it is in most other walks of life. For example, I have observed in the local game laws where I live the number of quail allowed in each season's bag. As my good fortune permits me to be in the field most of the time, I can make a fairly responsible report. Hunters speak nobly about eating, not wasting, what they kill. Correct, right down to the last creature on the endangered list. It is now thirty-seven years since I heard the bobwhite call, or since seeing the last one in this general area. Yet, the bag limit still holds out for a certain number of quail to be taken each season. Is this "intelligent harvesting" of our wildlife a fraudulent measure to dupe hunters for revenue, a tourist attraction, or simply our "best" standard of conservation? Since I have considered the utterly ridiculous forest "control" method of "multiple use" in another volume, I will not point it up here except to say that unless the wilderness areas we hope to save are legislated on a basis of the term *left inviolate*, instead of the term *multiple use*, we are heading for devastation of our most priceless resource.

Is it possible to find inviolate wilderness regions now which will remain so for tomorrow? I offer as an encouraging answer the following "Plea for a Paradise," which I wrote for the Alaska Area Director, Bureau of Sport Fisheries and Wildlife at Anchorage, Alaska. It might serve to give the reader a moral lift. The article appeared in the *Capital Magazine* of the St. Paul Sunday Pioneer Press, January 23, 1972, from which I quote the following:

Let's suppose for a moment that in the United States with its onrushing population increases, there is a wilderness area of nearly a million acres that has been left just about as wild and untrammeled as it was a thousand years ago. In the play of our imagination consider that only the rare individual has ever visited this grand expanse of nature. Further to improve our hypothesis consider that it has the most beautiful crater lakes in the world, set in spectacular mountains from which flow numerous cold mountain streams. To give the streams greater interest, punctuate their routes to the sea with scenically awesome waterfalls. To cap off the physiological nature of the almost million acres, add to its magnificent coastline 200 or more miles of wide sandy beach.

So much for its physiological features. To complete the wilderness paradise, suppose that we also add about 25 species of wild mammals, bears, wolves, fox, otter, wolverine, and members of the deer family. And in order to make a long coast fascinating beyond words, throw in a population of seals, sea lions, and other deep sea creatures. In our generosity, let's add geese by the tens of thousands, whistling

Include the deer family—Barren Ground Caribou.

Add to the list the red fox.

swans, ducks galore; even throw in a generous share of eider ducks and scoters. We might as well go all out and add cormorants, kittiwakes, murres, shearwaters for the shores; for the uplands, ptarmigan and songbirds. And we can't afford to leave out the bald eagle. Here in this natural wonderland, we will not consider him, as we must in other areas, an endangered species.

Incredible even to the imagination? It seems so today. It's like the fellow who said, "Imagine it: a thick steak, salad, baked potato, beverage and dessert all for thirty-five cents." A bystander remarked, "Where can I get this meal for thirty-five cents?" The reply, "I don't know, but just imagine it!"

". . . let's add geese by the tens of thousands . . ."

Go all out and
include the
Arctic tern.

Include rock ptarmigan.

"We can't afford to
leave out the bald
eagle."

"... *ducks galore* ..."

Should we be as facetiously speculative about the dream wilderness described? It is a wonderful prospect, but who is interested in an imaginative wilderness wonderland? Where in a world environment caught up in an industrial obsessionism could we imagine such an area?

We don't have to imagine it. It actually does exist. Every phase described above is factual on Unimak Island—the first, largest, and nearest to Alaska of the Aleutian chain. In fact, Unimak is so close to the Alaskan Peninsula, it seems almost to touch it.

It is quite true that many people living today and generations to come, may not in their lives observe an area of inviolate wilderness. This can become a serious cultural degeneration in any civilization. We could arrive at such ecological disaster in a relatively short time only by neglect.

Unimak, of course, is a long way off from most states, but it is, we need to remind ourselves, a part of the United States, which makes travel to it a lot more technically feasible. A journey to Unimak can be as enriching as the arrival itself, since travel en route is through that part of the North American continent possessing some of the most magnificent scenery. In a jet flight age, distance no longer poses the problem it once did. To leave a hurly-burly world of business and industry to arrive at an inviolate wilderness paradise, to camp, hike, climb, pick berries in endless profusion, beachcomb on hundreds of miles of sandy beach, fish, study nature, observe and photograph wildlife, ought to hold enchantment enough.

Once you as citizen help to preserve Unimak as a wilderness by law, some practical means of travel to the island will, no doubt, be provided. Right now it lies there a bit inaccessible in all its pristine grandeur, waiting for you and me to act.

The Unimak Island Wilderness Proposal has now had a complete hearing in Alaska by all principals concerned, and was reviewed by the Fish & Wildlife Service, Bureau of Sport Fisheries & Wildlife, U.S. Department of the Interior. The summary has also been sent up to the Secretary of the Interior. After his review, a proposal and statement supporting the action recommended will be sent to the President. After he reviews the proposal and is satisfied, he will send a proposal to Congress, who will make the final decision.

Tomorrow's wilderness thus holds promise. Those areas already set aside, and others like Unimak to be set aside, are probably some of the brightest precursors of what an awakening civilization holds for the future.